UNITED

PACKED WITH INFORMATION ON THE RED DEVILS

This edition published and distributed by Parragon, 1998

Parragon
Unit 13-17 Avonbridge Trading Estate
Atlantic Road
Avonmouth
Bristol BS11 9QD

Produced by Magpie Books,
an imprint of Robinson Publishing Ltd, London

ISBN 0 75252 550 6

A copy of the British Library Cataloguing-in-Publication
Data is available from the British Library.

Printed and bound in the EC.

This independent publication has been prepared without any
involvement on the part of Manchester United Football
Club or the FA Premier League.

UNITED

PACKED WITH INFORMATION ON THE RED DEVILS

Graham Betts

P

· PARRAGON ·

FACTFILE
UNITED

CONTENTS

INTRODUCTION

Little can be said about Manchester United that hasn't already appeared in books, newspapers and on the broadcast media. They are quite simply the greatest football club in the world today – a statement others will have a hard job contradicting.

Having captured the sympathy of the nation in 1958 when their great team of 'Busby Babes' was decimated in a plane crash, United won the adoration of the football world a decade later when the European Cup was won in entertaining and emphatic fashion. Three more decades have passed since that legendary victory, and though they have been far from universally successful the 1990s have seen United make the Premiership trophy their own personal possession.

By dividing United's history into easily digestible sections, this book seeks to inform and entertain. It cannot by its very size be exhaustive, and it is hoped that anyone fascinated by the facts and figures will purchase one of the weighty club histories available or follows United's match-by-match progress through the *Rothmans Football Yearbook*, published annually.

In these pages, however, you'll find details of the great players and double acts, the managers profiled together with their achievements, quotes, statistics, dream teams, month-by-month milestones…in short, much of what has gone to make this club a football institution.

GOALS GALORE!

It is often said that while good goals can be scored in almost any game, a truly great goal can only be scored on a big occasion – a goal that wins the Cup will be remembered long after a consolation effort.

Bobby Charlton undoubtedly scored many good goals during his career, but his truly great strikes in a United shirt probably came during the European Cup Final. However, his thunderous 30-yarder against Spurs during the 1965–66 clash at Old Trafford, or at Anfield a couple of seasons later, were possibly better-executed goals than either at Wembley.

David Beckham has developed into one of the top midfield players in the country and has proved time and again that he can weigh in with vital goals. Perhaps the pick of his ever-growing bunch was the outrageous strike from inside his own half at Selhurst Park against Wimbledon on the opening day of the 1996–97 season, a feat which settled the Goal of the Season contest in the shortest possible time!

Not surprisingly, Charlton holds most of United's individual records, topping the list for most League appearances in a red shirt (606), League goals in a career (199, the eight he subsequently scored for Preston taking him over the magical 200 mark) and most international caps (106). The record for most goals in a season, however, is held by Dennis Viollet, who bagged 32 goals in his 36 League appearances in the 1959-60 season. Dennis also bagged four in United's record Cup win, a 10-0 victory over RSC Anderlecht in the Preliminary Round of the 1956-57 European Cup, with Tommy Taylor scoring a hat-trick, Bill Whelan a brace and Johnny Berry a single strike.

Perhaps the best example of goalscoring in one game was provided by the mercurial George Best in the 1969-70 FA Cup Fifth Round clash at Northampton. Although the Cobblers were languishing mid-table in the Fourth Division and had struggled to get past Weymouth, Exeter City, Brentwood and Tranmere Rovers on their way, the prospect of a possible Cup upset had drawn a capacity crowd to the County Ground, with the pitch also likely to suit the home side more than the visitors.

As it was, Best chose this occasion to return to top form, scoring an astonishing six goals and running the show almost entirely. Two additional strikes by Brian Kidd and two replies from the home side left the final score 8-2 in United's favour, but it was Best who got all the headlines the following morning. In more recent times the best goalscoring performance by an individual is Andy Cole's five goals in one game against Ipswich Town in the Premier League in 1995, United going on to win 9-0.

But for an upheld complaint about their pitch at Bank Lane, Clayton, the record win for Newton Heath (the predecessors of Manchester United) would have been the 14-0 they registered over Walsall in the Second Division match in March 1895. After the game Walsall complained to the Football League, with the result the game was ordered to be replayed the following month. This time the Heathens could only manage nine!

In recent years the emerging goalscoring prowess of goalkeeper Peter Schmeichel has raised eyebrows; during the UEFA Cup campaign of 1995-96 United found themselves 2-0 down against Rotor Volgograd after only 24 minutes. This prompted an all-out charge on the attack, and Paul Scholes reduced the deficit with just over half an hour left on the clock.

As time ticked away and United faced defeat, Peter began to make an appearance in the opponents' penalty area whenever United had a corner. His presence alone ensured panic, but when he rose in the 89th minute and headed home the equaliser the roof was raised off Old Trafford. Although United went out of the competition on away goals, it showed Schmeichel contributed more to the team than just stopping goals; he could weigh in with one or two of his own at the opposite end as well!

There was no such thing as a lost cause as far as he was concerned, and in 1996-97 he once again appeared to have got himself on the scoresheet when a spectacular bicycle kick that Mark Hughes would have been proud of against Wimbledon in an FA Cup replay appeared to have rescued his team. Sadly, it was ruled out for offside.

While the days of one player contributing over 30 goals in a season would appear to be long gone, it is the prowess of United across the entire team that makes them such a threat. Fourteen different players got on the score sheet during United's 1996-97 Championship win, a further five goals being credited as own goals. This implies United are quicker than most teams in putting the opposing defence under pressure.

THROUGH THE YEARS
JANUARY

1910
January
22

United played their last match at their ground at Clayton, signing off with a 5-0 win over Spurs. Shortly after that match, one of the stands blew down!

1994
January
20

Sir Matt Busby died in hospital at the age of 84. Born in Orbiston in Scotland in 1909, he joined Manchester City in 1928 and helped the club to win the FA Cup in 1934 and a Scottish cap the same year against Wales. He was transferred to Liverpool in 1936 but saw his playing career cut short by the Second World War. Was offered a role on the Anfield coaching staff when the war ended but accepted instead the position of manager at Manchester United in October 1945.

Remained at the helm until 1969 when he became general manager, although took over the reins again in 1970 following the dismissal of Wilf McGuinness. During his spell United won five League titles, two FA Cups and in 1968 the European Cup. United's first match following his death, in the Premiership against Everton, saw a huge outpouring of emotion, with a lone Scottish piper leading the two teams out on to the pitch and a black ribbon being tied around the seat where Sir Matt Busby would normally have sat.

1995
January
10

One of the most surprising transfers of all time saw Andy Cole arrive at Old Trafford from Newcastle for £6 million in cash and Keith Gillespie making the opposite trip. That same month saw Eric Cantona sent off in the match at Selhurst Park and, as he was making his way to the dressing room, lash out at a fan. He was subsequently banned for eight months.

1975
January
21

Today saw the birth of future United and England midfielder Nicky Butt. A native Mancunian, he came up through the youth team alongside Giggs, Scholes and Beckham and has been acclaimed as the 'new Bryan Robson'.

1978
January
6

United have welcomed several ex-Leeds players into the fold over the years, notably Eric Cantona and Denis Irwin. Today though saw centre-forward Joe 'Jaws' Jordan sign for £350,000 – and he would mark his second Manchester derby appearance later in the year with the winning goal.

DREAM TEAM 1

Although this line-up is ostensibly from 1956-57, the side remained similar as United won successive titles and reached Wembley. By 1957-58 they had made progress in both the League and Europe, but the Munich air crash ended that dream. A patched-up United made it back to the Cup Final, but further bad luck meant runners-up medals were all they had to show for their efforts.

WOOD
1

FOULKES
2

COLMAN
4

JONES
5

BYRNE
3

BERRY
7

WHELAN
8

EDWARDS
6

PEGG
11

TAYLOR
9

VIOLLET
10

Goalkeeper   Ray Wood

Born in Hebburn-on-Tyne and signed for United as an 18-year-old in 1949, initially as cover for Jack Compton and then Reg Allen. Became a first-team regular in 1954 and survived the Munich air crash but by the time he had recovered from his injuries had lost his place to Harry Gregg.

Right-back   Bill Foulkes

Born in St Helens, he turned professional with United in 1951 and gave the club nearly 20 years sterling service. One of only two survivors of the Munich air crash to play in the first game after the disaster, the other being reserve keeper Harry Gregg. Appeared in the 1968 European Cup Final.

Left-back   Roger Byrne

A stylish and versatile player usually found at left back who could also play equally well on the left wing. Signed for United in 1949 and replaced Johnny Carey as captain. A member of three Championship-winning sides: 1952, 1956 and 1957. Killed in the Munich air disaster.

Right-half   Eddie Colman

A product of United's youth team, he made three winning appearances in the FA Youth Cup before going on to make his first-team debut in 1955. Although he was only 21 at the time he was killed at Munich, he had already won two Championship medals.

Centre-half   Mark Jones

Signed professional forms in 1950 and made his debut shortly after, becoming a permanent fixture in the side by 1955. Although he won two Championship medals, he briefly lost his place to Jackie Blanchflower for the FA Cup Final in 1957, but regained it later the same year. Died at Munich.

Left-half   Duncan Edwards

In an all-too-short career, Duncan achieved much in the game and was well on his way to becoming the finest player of his age. Like Eddie Colman he was only 21 when he died, but he had won two Championship medals, 18 England caps and had made his United debut at the age of 16 (he signed for the club two hours after turning 16). His strength and courage kept him alive for two weeks after the Munich crash, but he subsequently died from his injuries.

Outside-right   Johnny Berry

Born in Aldershot and began his career with Birmingham City, his performance in a match against United prompting Matt Busby to sign him as replacement for Johnny Delaney in 1951. Along with Roger Byrne, he won three Championship medals with United, although he was forced to retire following the injuries he received in the Munich air crash.

Inside-right   Billy (Liam) Whelan

Joined United from Home Farm in 1953 and played almost 100 games for the club over the next five years, although his best season was 1956-57 when he played in all but three of the

League games. At the time of Munich, he and Bobby Charlton were contesting the inside-right position, and, although Whelan did not play in that game against Red Star Belgrade, he was part of the squad and among those killed.

Centre-forward   Tommy Taylor
Began his career with Barnsley in 1949 and switched to Old Trafford in 1953 for £29,999, going on to make just short of 200 appearances for the first team. His goalscoring record was exceptional, with 128 goals scored for United and 16 for England from only 19 appearances. In Europe he managed 11 goals in only 14 starts and would surely have added to that tally had he not been killed at Munich.

Inside-left   Dennis Viollet
Locally born, he joined United as a 16-year-old and made his debut during the 1952-53 season, going on to serve the club for nine seasons. He holds the record for the most number of goals scored in a season, 32 in 1959-60, and was an integral part of the side that won successive Championships. Survived the Munich crash but missed most of the rest of the season. Left United for Stoke in 1962.

Outside-left   David Pegg
Made his debut for United shortly after his 17th birthday and was something of a regular in the two Championship-winning sides, although he had lost his place to Albert Scanlon at the time of the Munich crash, where he tragically lost his life.

APPEARANCES

As mentioned earlier, Bobby Charlton holds the record for the most League appearances in a United shirt, appearing in 606 League games between 1956 and 1973.

He made his debut on 6 October 1956 at home to Charlton Athletic (most appropriate!) and scored twice in the 4-2 win, going on to make 14 appearances and scoring ten goals in the season United retained the League title. It was not, however, until the 1958-59 season that he firmly established himself as a regular in the United side, making 21 appearances the following term (he obviously missed a considerable number of games while he recovered from injuries sustained in the Munich plane crash).

Thereafter, Bobby Charlton was perhaps one of the first names Matt Busby put on his team sheet for the next decade and a half. He made his final competitive appearance for United in the 1-0 defeat at Stamford Bridge against Chelsea on 28 April 1973, the home side making a presentation to him before the game in honour of his achievements. Interestingly enough, brother Jack also made his final League appearance on the same day away at Southampton for Leeds United.

It is, of course, purely hypothetical, but had it not been for Munich then all of the records held by Bobby Charlton would surely have belonged to Duncan Edwards. He made his debut for United at the age of 16 (a 4-1 reverse at Cardiff) while still an amateur and was almost ever-present for the next five years or so, racking up a total of 151 League appearances. He was the youngest player to play for England since the Second World War, an inspirational player who had already won 18 England caps and two Championship medals at the time of his death. While the ultimate European honour was finally achieved a little over ten years after the Munich disaster, there can be no doubt that, had he lived, Duncan would have been an integral part of that side.

The emergence of a classic crop of youngsters in recent years might indicate that Charlton's record could one day be under threat, but Alex Ferguson has quickly learned that football in the 1990s is completely different from football of even ten years ago; it is now a squad game, with players being picked to do a specific job within a specific game and even the greats are not guaranteed a regular place in the starting line-up. Even so, Ryan Giggs – the first fledgling to benefit from Fergie's protecting hand – still managed to amass over 200 League appearances by the time he was 24 and could, if he avoids injury and the allure of playing elsewhere, get close to Charlton's record in about ten years!

Others have worn the United shirt for considerably less time; the great Peter Beardsley, who made his name with Newcastle United, Liverpool, Everton and Newcastle again, made but one appearance for Manchester United during his six months with the club following his transfer from Vancouver Whitecaps, at home to Bournemouth in the Second Round first leg of the League Cup in 1982 and was substituted by Frank Stapleton. He then returned to Vancouver to begin picking up the pieces of his career.

At least he has that one game to look back on – something that proved beyond future England captain David Platt, given a free transfer to Crewe before making even one appearance for United's first team! Another of United's promising youngsters, Pat McGibbon, has actually made more appearances for the Northern Ireland first team (five) than for United, his one appearance also being a League Cup match!

THROUGH THE YEARS
FEBRUARY

1910
February

Manchester United moved to a brand new stadium at Old Trafford. The amenities for the players were superb – a billiard room, massage rooms, gymnasium, laundry and plunge bath. The ground held 80,000 spectators, with 13,000 under cover. Prices at the ground were six old pence for admission to the terraces, one shilling, one shilling and sixpence and two shillings to the covered stand, and five shillings for a reserved seat in the centre of the stand (where attendants directed patrons to their tip-up seats!).

1958
February
6

The worst disaster in United's history, the Munich air crash, wiped out a side that might have won the European Cup. United had played Red Star Belgrade and drawn 3-3 to book their place in the Semi-Final of the competition. On the flight back home the plane, an Elizabethan airliner, made a refuelling stop at Munich, where it was snowing heavily. The plane made two aborted attempts at take off and on the third fateful run is believed to have clipped a house at the end of the runway and burst into flames.

Those who died immediately included players Roger Byrne, Eddie Colman, Liam Whelan, Tommy Taylor, David Pegg (who all played in the last season's FA Cup Final), Mark Jones and Geoff Bent, club secretary Walter Crickmer, coach Bert Whalley and trainer Tom Curry, two crew members, two other passengers and eight journalists, including former England goalkeeper Frank Swift, of the *News Of The World*.

Matt Busby and Duncan Edwards were both reported to be close to death (Duncan fought a vain but very brave battle for almost two weeks), with Busby giving most cause for concern having suffered a crushed chest and having the last rites read to him. The injuries suffered by Johnny Berry and Jackie Blanchflower were such they did not play again.

1945
February
15

Company Sergeant-Major Matt Busby, whose footballing career included a spell at Maine Road, was appointed United's first postwar manager. Unfortunately, though hostilities in Europe had ceased, it would still take time for him to return to civvy street and the Old Trafford board had to wait for his demob – but who can say it wasn't worth it?

1996
February
25

A short trip to Burnden Park saw Premiership newcomers Bolton crushed 6-0. The win marked United's last month in second place behind Newcastle: the Magpies lost their nerve and the Red Devils powered to the title.

GREAT STRIKERS

Goals win prizes – and, with such a collection of silverware over the years, it's hardly suprising that United have been blessed with more than their share of fine forwards.

 ## BOBBY CHARLTON

During the course of his long and illustrious career, Bobby Charlton won just about every honour the game had to offer. More importantly, he did everything with a sense of sportsmanship that had not been seen before or since. He was and still is the perfect ambassador for the game.

Born in Ashington on 11 October 1937 he was a relative of the Milburn family and as such was a football prodigy as a schoolboy, representing England at schoolboy and youth level before signing professional forms with Manchester United.

However, before he broke into the first team he played his part in helping United win three consecutive FA Youth Cups. He made his debut for United's first team in October 1956 and scored twice against Charlton, playing moderately regularly in the side the following season. He survived the Munich air crash and then became an integral part of the side as Matt Busby had to build from scratch.

After helping United to the FA Cup in 1963 and two League titles, he played a major part in ensuring the European Cup came to Old Trafford in 1968, scoring two goals in the

Final against Benfica. He was first capped for England in 1958 against Scotland and went on to win a then record 106 caps, including an appearance in the 1966 World Cup Final. Indeed, his performances during that tournament lifted him from United icon to national treasure, particularly in the Semi-Final against Portugal when it was his two goals that took England into the Final. He has scored more goals for England than any other player – 49, and is also United's record goalscorer.

He was awarded an OBE in 1969, later collected a CBE and in 1994 was made a knight. As a player his individual honours included the Football Writers' Player of the Year and European Player of the Year in 1966.

He retired as a player at the end of the 1972-73 season, but was tempted back when Preston, the club he left to manage, had need of his inspirational qualities on as well as off the field. He later became a United director.

BOBBY CHARLTON UNITED RECORD 1956-73									
League		FA Cup		League Cup		Europe		Total	
Apps	Goals	Apps	Goals	Apps	Goals	Apps	Goals	Apps	Goals
606	199	79	19	24	7	45	22	754	247

DENIS LAW

In his ten seasons with Manchester United, Denis Law enjoyed a strike rate better than perhaps any other player who has worn the red shirt. All of this will be no surprise to those who first witnessed his introduction to League football back in 1957, for the bespectacled 16-year-old youngster looked anything but a professional footballer. However, once he put on his kit and got in front of goal, there were few better.

Born in Aberdeen on 24 February 1940, he was signed for Huddersfield Town by Bill Shankly while still a schoolboy, quickly developing into a feared striker. He was snapped up by Manchester City in March 1960 for £55,000, then a League record, and his year or so with City is perhaps best remembered for the occasion he scored six goals in a Cup tie at Luton only for the game to be abandoned! He also scored in the replayed match, but City lost 3–1…

In July 1961, Torino offered City a record fee of £100,000, but like Jimmy Greaves he struggled to adjust to life in Italy and a year later returned to Manchester, this time for United, for £115,000. He was an instant hit at Old Trafford, helping United win the FA Cup in their first season, including scoring in the Final against Leicester City. He then went on to help United lift two League titles – but just as Greaves missed the match his career had been building towards, the World Cup Final, so Denis missed out on United's greatest triumph, the 1968 European Cup Final, watching the match on television while in hospital.

Being voted European Player of the Year in 1964 was scant compensation, although he was also selected for the Rest of the World side in 1963 against England and scored their goal in the 2–1 defeat. In July 1973 he rejoined City where he spent one final season. Ironically, he scored the goal at Old Trafford which confirmed United's relegation to the Second Division and, demoralised, hung up his boots immediately.

Although Bobby Charlton holds the honours as United's greatest goalscorer, the efforts of Denis Law, who played considerably fewer matches, should not be overlooked. He was capped 55 times for Scotland, scoring 30 goals.

DENIS LAW UNITED RECORD 1962-73									
League		FA Cup		League Cup		Europe		Total	
Apps	Goals	Apps	Goals	Apps	Goals	Apps	Goals	Apps	Goals
309	171	46	34	11	3	33	28	399	236

GEORGE BEST

George Best's reputation as one of the finest players ever seen since the Second World War is assured, but there will forever be a feeling he could and should have achieved much more in the game he graced. The pressures suffered by modern day footballers were nothing when compared to those endured by George Best, and there is much in his career that can serve as a vital lesson to his modern-day counterparts.

Born in Belfast on 22 May 1946, he was recommended to United as a 15-year-old schoolboy but soon after his arrival was homesick and it took almost constant persuasion from Busby to ensure George's continued presence in Manchester. He made his debut for United in September 1963 and after only 15 League appearances was selected by Northern Ireland, winning the first of his 37 caps against Wales.

It was his club form, however, that earned most of the accolades, none more so than his superb individual performance in the European Cup tie in Lisbon against Benfica in March 1966 which earned the nickname 'El Beatle'; perhaps the signal for George Best adulation to reach fever pitch. He helped United win the title in 1965 and 1967 and the following season was an integral member of the side that lifted the European Cup, scoring in the Final against, ironically enough, Benfica.

Following Sir Matt Busby's resignation George's career went into decline, not least because the player was no longer prepared to handle the pressure fame and fortune had brought him, and after several disappearances he announced his intention to retire in 1974. He subsequently turned out for Stockport County, Fulham, Bournemouth and Hibernian, as well as appearing in America and elsewhere.

It is perhaps one of the tragedies of football that this undoubted genius never graced a major international tournament; he might have helped Northern Ireland in 1982 when they qualified for Spain, but manager Billy Bingham ignored sentiment and left George behind. As his side made the Quarter-Finals, who is to say he was wrong? George was named Footballer of the Year and European Footballer of the Year in 1968, a period that was undoubtedly his heyday.

GEORGE BEST UNITED RECORD 1963-74									
League		FA Cup		League Cup		Europe		Total	
Apps	Goals	Apps	Goals	Apps	Goals	Apps	Goals	Apps	Goals
361	137	46	21	25	9	34	11	466	178

ANDY COLE

When Alex Ferguson signed Andy Cole from Newcastle United in January 1995 it was a transfer that stunned the whole of football. Indeed, it is difficult to imagine a more surprising move in recent years, for it seemed as though Andy would be an integral part of Newcastle's attempts to unseat United as Champions for some considerable time.

Born in Nottingham on 15 October 1971, he signed as a trainee with Arsenal in 1989 and was later upgraded to the professional ranks. After two substitute appearances and a brief loan spell with Fulham, he was sold to Bristol City in 1992 for £500,000 – a figure which seems on the low side, bearing in mind the fees he has since commanded.

His form at Bristol City was little short of sensational, 20 goals coming in his 41 League appearances for the Ashton Gate outfit, and a move to Newcastle United followed in March 1993 for £1.75 million. At St James' Park the decision was taken to build the side around his striking qualities, and Andy responded well to the responsibility, scoring 55 goals in 70 appearances (including one as a substitute).

Whether Kevin Keegan had been alerted that Alan Shearer was likely to be sold and needed to raise sufficient funds for that swoop we will never know, but when it was announced Andy was being sold for £7 million (a figure made up of £6 million in cash and Keith Gillespie being valued at £1 million) to Manchester United, the football world sat up and took notice.

It took Andy some time to settle in at Old Trafford. While Newcastle had played to his strengths, he was now just another player who had to slot into a system that had worked well for the previous five years or so. However, once he had settled in, he began scoring goals at an alarming rate again. Keegan may well have landed Alan Shearer, but in so doing he unleashed a prolific goalscorer in a side that already scores goals for fun!

ANDY COLE UNITED RECORD 1995-(97)									
League		FA Cup		League Cup		Europe		Total	
Apps	Goals	Apps	Goals	Apps	Goals	Apps	Goals	Apps	Goals
72	30	10	2	1	—	6	1	89	33

BEST SEASON 1

The appointment of Matt Busby as manager
of United at the end of the Second World
War proved to be a masterstroke, for by
1948 he had led the club to success in the
FA Cup and four years later had brought
home the League title. The 1956–57 season
saw United consolidating their position as
kings of England.

Almost as soon as the title was in the bag, Busby set about
rebuilding the club, placing his faith on a conveyor-belt
of young players who were evolving out of the youth
team. United would win the first five FA Youth Cup Finals (a
run which began in the 1952–53 season), many of the players
who helped keep the trophy at Old Trafford going on to
become first-team regulars, including Duncan Edwards,
Eddie Colman and Bobby Charlton; playing together on a
regular basis for the youth team benefited United when those
same players broke into the first team.

By the time the 1955–56 season came around, the United
team had effectively grown up together; their ability to gel
was almost telepathic. Although the season began with two
draws and three defeats in the opening nine games, thereafter
the team began to get into their stride and opened up a
sizeable lead at the head of the table. While Busby had been
there before, most of his team had not, but he was astute
enough to juggle the team around, resting players before they
became jaded, keeping competition for places keen and
motivating his players to attain heights they had previously

only dreamed of, and keep the momentum going.

By the end of the season, United had suffered only a further four defeats to register just seven throughout, all of which were received at opponents' grounds. Unbeaten at home they dropped only three points all season at Old Trafford and won the title by an astonishing 11 points from Blackpool and Wolves, with both Tommy Taylor and Dennis Viollet netting over 20 goals during the season (Taylor 25, Viollet 20). A Third Round defeat at Bristol Rovers in the FA Cup (by 4-0) had been the only blip on the horizon, but by winning the League title United became eligible for the European Cup, a competition Matt Busby would ignore Football Association and Football League advice to enter. The march towards eventual success in 1968 began here.

1955-56 LEAGUE RECORD		
Opponents	**Home**	**Away**
Arsenal	1-1	1-1
Aston Villa	1-0	4-4
Birmingham City	2-1	2-2
Blackpool	2-1	0-0
Bolton Wanderers	1-0	1-3
Burnley	2-0	0-0
Cardiff City	1-1	1-0
Charlton Athletic	5-1	0-3
Chelsea	3-0	4-2
Everton	2-1	2-4
Huddersfield Town	3-0	2-0
Luton Town	3-1	2-0
Manchester City	2-1	0-1
Newcastle United	5-2	0-0
Portsmouth	1-0	2-3
Preston North End	3-2	1-3
Sheffield United	3-1	0-1
Sunderland	2-1	2-2
Tottenham Hotspur	2-2	2-1
West Bromwich Albion	3-1	4-1
Wolverhampton Wanderers	4-3	2-0

DERBY 📷 FOCUS

Derby matches between Manchester City and United have a special flavour all of their own which few outsiders can fully understand. Given the respective standing of the two clubs, it is surprising they have never contested a major Cup Final, have had probably only one League match vital to both their title aspirations and have only met in the FA Charity Shield once.

The original forerunners of Manchester City were West Gorton who formed in 1880 and merged with Gorton Athletic in 1887 to become Ardwick FC. Indeed, it was as Ardwick that the very first Manchester derby match took place, an FA Cup Qualifying Round fixture played on 3 October 1891 at Newton Heath's North Road ground. The two clubs marked the special occasion by inviting local politician Sir James Ferguson to kick off a fixture that has gone on to become one of the most eagerly awaited days in the Manchester football calendar. The Heathens recorded a 5-1 win – and while the balance of control within the city has ebbed and flowed, current form has seldom counted for anything when the two sides clash.

Leaving aside the Football Alliance meetings, the clubs' first official League meeting took place three years after that initial FA Cup tie, the Heathens maintaining their supremacy over their rivals with a 5-2 win at City's (they changed their name to Manchester City in 1894) Hyde Road ground. City's two goals on a day they would rather forget were scored by one of the most illustrious names on the Manchester football scene, Billy Meredith.

It would not be an understatement to say that Meredith almost single-handedly put Manchester on the football map during the game's early, formative years, giving sterling service to both clubs during his career. In 1912 the League clash between the two sides at Old Trafford was played as a benefit for Meredith, with the player picking up gate receipts of over £2,000. What no one in the 40,000 crowd could have expected was that Billy would still be playing in City and United derbies in 1921!

While Newton Heath (they did not change their name to Manchester United until 1902) had the upper hand in the opening few years, City were the first club to bring some major silverware back home to Manchester, winning the FA Cup in 1904 and might have gone on to establish a footballing dynasty within the city but for an illegal payments scandal which rocked the club in 1906. As a result, 17 players were banned on the orders of the Football Association from May 1906 until 1907 and the club were forced to play reserves in their place.

City might have been able to survive this blow had it not been for United manager Ernest Mangnall persuading five of the players, including Billy Meredith and Sandy Turnbull, to swap the blue of City for the red of United. Within two years, United had won their first League Championship and the following year the FA Cup.

The first time the two clubs met in a truly vital match was in 1926 when they were paired in the FA Cup Semi-Final. While the whole city had hoped and prayed the clubs could avoid each other until the Wembley showpiece, Bolton drew Swansea and so Manchester had to content itself with its own private Cup Final to be played at Sheffield United's Bramall Lane. United were expected to win for, while they were settled in mid-table security, City were involved in an unsuccessful fight against relegation.

Form, not for the first time, went out of the window, for United appeared nervous when the two clubs strode out on to the pitch and City were quick to take advantage. A hotly disputed goal in the 14th minute in City's favour settled the Blues and seemed to cause United's heads to drop.

Frank Barson then went on one of his customary headless strolls, crashing into Sam Cowan and earning a stiff lecture from the referee. Thereafter he was not the same player and City scored two further goals to book their place at Wembley. There, just as in 1904, they would meet Bolton Wanderers, but this time the Trotters gained revenge and the trophy with a 1-0 win.

The League meeting between the two at Old Trafford on 7 February 1931 saw the one and only Manchester derby appearance by the great Matt Busby – but it will surprise many to learn that he appeared not in the home side dressing room but the visitors', inspiring City to a 3-1 win and helping to push United a step nearer relegation! As a result, it would be a five years before the two clubs met in League battle again, with honours over the season finishing equal – United winning 3-2 at home while City triumphed 1-0 at Maine Road.

More importantly, City ended the season as Champions, while United were relegated back into the Second Division! And, just to show how bizarre football can be, the following season United made an immediate return to the First Division as runners up to Aston Villa while City were relegated, the first time the reigning Champions had been demoted!

When League football took an enforced break owing to the Second World War and Old Trafford was put out of action thanks to heavy German bombing, it was to Maine Road that United turned for salvation and assistance, City turning over their facilities to their greatest rivals on a shared basis.

By the turn of the 1950s there were two great sides being built across the city; United's emerging Busby Babes would sweep almost all before them until decimated at Munich, while City's followers had their own success to cheer about, including the FA Cup in 1956. A year previously City had recorded one of their finest victories over their rivals with a 5-0 hammering at Old Trafford. This match is particularly worthy of mention, for the key to City's success was the use of Don Revie as a midfield schemer rather than the out and out centre-forward the shirt number he wore (Number 9) seemed to indicate.

While players today wear squad numbers that do not always relate to positions, up until the mid 1960s the number on a player's shirt seemed to be a strait-jacket; the Number 2 played at left-back, the Number 7 on the right wing and so on. So if the Number 9 (Revie) dropped back, the centre-half was caught in two minds as to whether to follow him. Among the confusion, Revie picked out his team-mates with ease and enabled City to record one of their biggest wins over their rivals.

City's success in the following season's FA Cup and United's League title triumph pitched both clubs into their first and so far only FA Charity Shield meeting. What has since gone on to become a traditional season curtain-raiser in front of a full Wembley crowd was played on a cold October evening at Maine Road, although tradition indicated that United should have had home advantage as Champions. The reason for the game being switched to Maine Road was because City had floodlights, while United were still in the process of installing their system. As it was, home advantage counted for little as Dennis Viollet grabbed the only goal of the game in the 75th minute to ensure a further trophy for the United boardroom.

The intense rivalry between the two clubs was forgotten in the immediate aftermath of the Munich air disaster. Although it was the bulk of the United team that perished, City sustained their own loss with the death of former goalkeeper turned journalist Frank Swift and joined their rivals in mourning.

It took United time to rebuild, finally emerging with a team capable of living with the best in the mid 1960s, at pretty much the same time City had also rebuilt and regrouped. City, managed by Joe Mercer and coached by Malcolm Allison, seemed to get the upper hand, winning 3-1 at Old Trafford in late March 1968 on their way to winning the League Championship for only the second time in the club's history. That they pipped their nearest rivals by two points made the victory ultimately all the more sweet, but United would gain more than adequate compensation with victory in the European Cup Final.

While the two sides were drawn in the League Cup Semi-Final in 1969, with City winning on aggregate and picking up the trophy after beating West Bromwich Albion, the next truly important match between the two sides was the League clash on the 27 April 1974. United were battling against relegation to the Second Division and the points were vital if they were to avoid the drop. And while City could be the side which condemned them to the Second Division for the first time since 1938, there was little indication during the first 85 minutes of conflict that their heart was really in it.

Then a cheeky flick from former United favourite Denis Law, playing in the blue of City, eluded Alex Stepney and prompted a pitch invasion by the United followers. In the bedlam that followed, the crowd ignored a loudspeaker appeal by Sir Matt Busby and forced the referee to take both sides off the field. The result was allowed to stand, Law hung up his boots and United were plunged into the Second Division.

While there has not been a match of such high drama since (or, to be honest, before) it does not detract from the rivalry between the two sides. United's current status as top dogs in

English football must rankle with the City followers more than anything, and a victory over their rivals is one to be savoured, regardless of whether it is a 1-0 win as in 1981 or a 5-1 win as in 1989 (City's last victory).

When City were relegated in 1996, United's record stood as follows:

Competition	P	W	D	L	F	A
Football League	125	49	44	32	183	166
FA Cup	6	4	—	2	11	7
League Cup	3	—	1	2	3	8
Charity Shield	1	1	—	—	1	—
Friendlies, War games etc	138	61	21	56	254	220
Total	**273**	**115**	**66**	**92**	**452**	**401**

With the Maine Road side currently languishing in the First Division, the whole of Manchester must wait for match-by-match rivalry to be resumed.

UNITED'S TOP 10 DERBY APPEARANCES			
1	Bobby Charlton	1956-73	27
2	Alex Stepney	1966-78	24
3	Bill Foulkes	1952-69	23
4	Martin Buchan	1972-82	20
5=	Steve Coppell	1975-83	17
5=	Sammy McIlroy	1971-82	17
7=	Arthur Albiston	1974-88	16
7=	Tony Dunne	1960-73	16
7=	Lou Macari	1973-83	16
10=	George Best	1963-74	15
10=	Roger Byrne	1951-58	15
10=	Billy Meredith	1906-21	15
10=	David Sadler	1963-73	15
10=	Nobby Stiles	1960-71	15
10=	Dennis Viollet	1952-71	15

THROUGH THE YEARS
MARCH

1995

March

4

Manchester United shatter the Premier League goalscoring record with a 9-0 whipping of relegation-bound Ipswich Town at Old Trafford. At the same time, record transfer buy Andy Cole grabbed five goals to become the first player to score as many in a Premier League match. It was also Manchester United's biggest League win since 1892, when they beat Wolves 10-1.

1966

March

9

George Best took centre stage today in Benfica's magnificent Stadium of Light, shattering the Portuguese Champions' proud record of 19 unbeaten European home games with a dazzling two-goal performance – and that in the first 45 minutes! The 5-1 result added to a 3-2 home win to take United to the Semi-Finals, and though they lost to Partizan Belgrade they would again meet and beat Benfica in the 1968 Final.

1983

March

26

Having brought the FA Cup back to Old Trafford four times, United reached the Final of the League Cup, then the Milk Cup, for the first time. Unfortunately, the period saw Liverpool lay claim to the trophy in perpetuity, and a 2-1 defeat, Norman Whiteside scoring, fell into the pattern. A fifth FA Cup win later this year would make up for the disappointment.

1963

March

4

After the big freeze had put football on hold for fully two months, United played their FA Cup Third Round match against Huddersfield today and made up for lost time by winning 5-0. Three more ties were played this month, United winning through to meet and beat Leicester in the Final.

1991

March

14

Recognising that the club have been restored to the peak of English football, the United board award Alex Ferguson a £1,000 a week pay rise as part of a new four-year contract. Within six years, he will bring four Championships to Old Trafford.

FA CUP RECORD

The quest for England's premier knockout trophy has created over a century of fixtures – all documented here.

Stage	Opponents	Score
1886-87		
Round 1	Fleetwood Rovers	2-2
Newton Heath lost on refusing to play extra time		
1887-88		
Did not enter		
1888-89		
Did not enter		
1889-90		
Round 1	Preston North End	1-6
1890-91		
Qualifier 1	Higher Walton	2-0
Qualifier 2	Bootle Reserves	0-1
1891-92		
Qualifier 1	Ardwick	5-1
Qualifier 2	Heywood	Walkover
Qualifier 3	South Shore	2-0
Qualifier 4	Blackpool	3-4

Stage	Opponents	Score
	1892-93	
Round 1	Blackburn Rovers	0-4
	1893-94	
Round 1	Middlesbrough	4-0
Round 2	Blackburn Rovers	0-0, 1-5
	1894-95	
Round 1	Stoke	2-3
	1895-96	
Round 1	Kettering Town	2-1
Round 2	Derby County	1-1, 1-5
	1896-97	
Qualifier 1	West Manchester	7-0
Qualifier 2	Nelson	3-0
Qualifier 3	Blackpool	2-2, 2-1
Round 1	Kettering Town	5-1
Round 2	Southampton	1-1, 3-1
Round 3	Derby County	0-2
	1897-98	
Round 1	Walsall	1-0
Round 2	Liverpool	0-0, 1-2
	1898-99	
Round 1	Tottenham Hotspur	1-1, 3-5
	1899-1900	
Qualifier 1	South Shore	1-3

Stage	Opponents	Score
1900-01		
Intermediate	Portsmouth	3-0
Round 1	Burnley	0-0, 1-7
1901-02		
Intermediate	Lincoln City	1-2
1902-03		
Qualifier 3	Accrington Stanley	7-0
Qualifier 4	Oswaldtwistle	3-2
Qualifier 5	Southport Central	4-1
Intermediate	Burton United	1-1, 3-1
Round 1	Liverpool	2-1
Round 2	Everton	1-3
1903-04		
Intermediate	Small Heath	1-1, 1-1, 1-1, 3-1
Round 1	Notts County	3-3, 2-1
Round 2	Sheffield Wednesday	0-6
1904-05		
Intermediate	Fulham	2-2, 0-0, 0-1
1905-06		
Round 1	Staple Hill	7-2
Round 2	Norwich City	3-0
Round 3	Aston Villa	5-1
Round 4	Woolwich Arsenal	2-3
1906-07		
Round 1	Portsmouth	2-2, 1-2

Stage	Opponents	Score
	1907-08	
Round 1	Blackpool	3-1
Round 2	Chelsea	1-0
Round 3	Aston Villa	2-0
Round 4	Fulham	1-2
	1908-09	
Round 1	Brighton & HA	1-0
Round 2	Everton	1-0
Round 3	Blackburn Rovers	6-1
Round 4	Burnley	0-1*, 3-2
Match abandoned after 72 minutes		
Semi-Final	Newcastle United	1-0
Final	Bristol City	1-0
	1909-10	
Round 1	Burnley	0-2
	1910-11	
Round 1	Blackpool	2-1
Round 2	Aston Villa	2-1
Round 3	West Ham United	1-2
	1911-12	
Round 1	Huddersfield Town	3-1
Round 2	Coventry City	5-1
Round 3	Reading	1-1, 3-0
Round 4	Blackburn Rovers	1-1, 2-4
	1912-13	
Round 1	Coventry City	1-1, 2-1
Round 2	Plymouth Argyle	2-0
Round 3	Oldham Athletic	0-0, 1-2

Stage	Opponents	Score
1913-14		
Round 1	Swindon Town	0-1
1914-15		
Round 1	Sheffield Wednesday	0-1
1919-20		
Round 1	Port Vale	1-0
Round 2	Aston Villa	1-2
1920-21		
Round 1	Liverpool	1-1, 1-2
1921-22		
Round 1	Cardiff City	1-4
1922-23		
Round 1	Bradford City	1-1, 2-0
Round 2	Tottenham Hotspur	0-4
1923-24		
Round 1	Plymouth Argyle	1-0
Round 2	Huddersfield Town	0-3
1924-25		
Round 1	Sheffield Wednesday	0-2
1925-26		
Round 3	Port Vale	3-2
Round 4	Tottenham Hotspur	2-2, 2-0
Round 5	Sunderland	3-3, 2-1
Round 6	Fulham	2-1
Semi-Final	Manchester City	0-3

Stage	Opponents	Score
1926-27		
Round 3	Reading	1-1, 2-2, 1-2
1927-28		
Round 3	Brentford	7-1
Round 4	Bury	1-1, 1-0
Round 5	Birmingham	1-0
Round 6	Blackburn Rovers	0-2
1928-29		
Round 3	Port Vale	3-0
Round 4	Bury	0-1
1929-30		
Round 3	Swindon Town	0-2
1930-31		
Round 3	Stoke City	3-3, 0-0, 4-2
Round 4	Grimsby Town	0-1
1931-32		
Round 3	Plymouth Argyle	1-4
1932-33		
Round 3	Middlesbrough	1-4
1933-34		
Round 3	Portsmouth	1-1, 1-4
1934-35		
Round 3	Bristol Rovers	3-1
Round 4	Nottingham Forest	0-0, 0-3

Stage	Opponents	Score
1935-36		
Round 3	Reading	3-1
Round 4	Stoke City	0-0, 0-2
1936-37		
Round 3	Reading	1-0
Round 4	Arsenal	0-5
1937-38		
Round 3	Yeovil	3-0
Round 4	Barnsley	2-2, 1-0
Round 5	Brentford	0-2
1938-39		
Round 3	West Bromwich Albion	0-0, 1-5
1945-46		
Round 3	Accrington Stanley	2-2, 5-1
Round 4	Preston North End	1-0, 1-3
1946-47		
Round 3	Bradford Park Avenue	3-0
Round 4	Nottingham Forest	0-2
1947-48		
Round 3	Aston Villa	6-4
Round 4	Liverpool	3-0
Round 5	Charlton Athletic	2-0
Round 6	Preston North End	4-1
Semi-Final	Derby County	3-1
Final	Blackpool	4-2

Stage	Opponents	Score
	1948-49	
Round 3	Bournemouth	6-0
Round 4	Bradford Park Avenue	1-1, 1-1, 5-0
Round 5	Yeovil Town	8-0
Round 6	Hull City	1-0
Semi-Final	Wolves	1-1, 0-1
	1949-50	
Round 3	Weymouth	4-0
Round 4	Watford	1-0
Round 5	Portsmouth	3-3, 3-1
Round 6	Chelsea	0-2
	1950-51	
Round 3	Oldham Athletic	4-1
Round 4	Leeds United	4-0
Round 5	Arsenal	1-0
Round 6	Birmingham City	0-1
	1951-52	
Round 3	Hull City	0-2
	1952-53	
Round 3	Millwall	1-0
Round 4	Walthamstow Avenue	1-1, 5-2
Round 5	Everton	1-2
	1953-54	
Round 3	Burnley	3-5
	1954-55	
Round 3	Reading	1-1, 4-1
Round 4	Manchester City	0-2

Stage	Opponents	Score
1955-56		
Round 3	Bristol Rovers	0-4
1956-57		
Round 3	Hartlepools United	4-3
Round 4	Wrexham	5-0
Round 5	Everton	1-0
Round 6	Bournemouth	2-1
Semi-Final	Birmingham City	2-0
Final	Aston Villa	1-2
1957-58		
Round 3	Workington	3-1
Round 4	Ipswich Town	2-0
Round 5	Sheffield Wednesday	3-0
Round 6	West Bromwich Albion	2-2, 1-0
Semi-Final	Fulham	2-2, 5-3
Final	Bolton Wanderers	0-2
1958-59		
Round 3	Norwich City	0-3
1959-60		
Round 3	Derby County	4-2
Round 4	Liverpool	3-1
Round 5	Sheffield Wednesday	0-1
1960-61		
Round 3	Middlesbrough	3-0
Round 4	Sheffield Wednesday	1-1, 2-7

Stage	Opponents	Score
1961-62		
Round 3	Bolton Wanderers	2-1
Round 4	Arsenal	1-0
Round 5	Sheffield Wednesday	0-0, 2-0
Round 6	Preston North End	0-0, 2-1
Semi-Final	Tottenham Hotspur	1-3
1962-63		
Round 3	Huddersfield Town	5-0
Round 4	Aston Villa	1-0
Round 5	Chelsea	2-1
Round 6	Coventry City	3-1
Semi-Final	Southampton	1-0
Final	Leicester City	3-1
1963-64		
Round 3	Southampton	3-2
Round 4	Bristol Rovers	4-1
Round 5	Barnsley	4-0
Round 6	Sunderland	3-3, 2-2, 5-1
Semi-Final	West Ham United	1-3
1964-65		
Round 3	Chester	2-1
Round 4	Stoke City	0-0, 1-0
Round 5	Burnley	2-1
Round 6	Wolves	5-3
Semi-Final	Leeds United	0-0, 0-1

Stage	Opponents	Score
	1965-66	
Round 3	Derby County	5-2
Round 4	Rotherham United	0-0, 1-0
Round 5	Wolves	4-2
Round 6	Preston North End	1-1, 3-1
Semi-Final	Everton	0-1
	1966-67	
Round 3	Stoke City	2-0
Round 4	Norwich City	1-2
	1967-68	
Round 3	Tottenham Hotspur	2-2, 0-1
	1968-69	
Round 3	Exeter City	3-1
Round 4	Watford	1-1, 2-0
Round 5	Birmingham City	2-2, 6-2
Round 6	Everton	0-1
	1969-70	
Round 3	Ipswich Town	1-0
Round 4	Manchester City	3-0
Round 5	Northampton Town	8-2
Round 6	Middlesbrough	1-1, 2-1
Semi-Final	Leeds United	0-0, 0-0, 0-1
3/4 play-off	Watford	2-0
	1970-71	
Round 3	Middlesbrough	0-0, 1-2

Stage	Opponents	Score
1971-72		
Round 3	Southampton	1-1, 4-1
Round 4	Preston North End	2-0
Round 5	Middlesbrough	0-0, 3-0
Round 6	Stoke City	1-1, 1-2
1972-73		
Round 3	Wolves	0-1
1973-74		
Round 3	Plymouth Argyle	1-0
Round 4	Ipswich Town	0-1
1974-75		
Round 3	Walsall	0-0, 2-3
1975-76		
Round 3	Oxford United	2-1
Round 4	Peterborough United	3-1
Round 5	Leicester City	2-1
Round 6	Wolves	1-1, 3-2
Semi-Final	Derby County	2-0
Final	Southampton	0-1
1976-77		
Round 3	Walsall	1-0
Round 4	Queens Park Rangers	1-0
Round 5	Southampton	2-2, 2-1
Round 6	Aston Villa	2-1
Semi-Final	Leeds United	2-1
Final	Liverpool	2-1

Stage	Opponents	Score
1977-78		
Round 3	Carlisle United	1-1, 4-2
Round 4	West Bromwich Albion	1-1, 2-3
1978-79		
Round 3	Chelsea	3-0
Round 4	Fulham	1-1, 1-0
Round 5	Colchester United	1-0
Round 6	Tottenham Hotspur	1-1, 2-0
Semi-Final	Liverpool	2-2, 1-0
Final	Arsenal	2-3
1979-80		
Round 3	Tottenham Hotspur	1-1, 0-1
1980-81		
Round 3	Brighton & HA	2-2, 2-0
Round 4	Nottingham Forest	0-1
1981-82		
Round 3	Watford	0-1
1982-83		
Round 3	West Ham United	2-0
Round 4	Luton Town	2-0
Round 5	Derby County	1-0
Round 6	Everton	1-0
Semi-Final	Arsenal	2-1
Final	Brighton & HA	2-2, 4-0
1983-84		
Round 3	Bournemouth	0-2

Stage	Opponents	Score
	1984-85	
Round 3	Bournemouth	3-0
Round 4	Coventry City	2-1
Round 5	Blackburn Rovers	2-0
Round 6	West Ham United	4-2
Semi-Final	Liverpool	2-2, 2-1
Final	Everton	1-0
	1985-86	
Round 3	Rochdale	2-0
Round 4	Sunderland	0-0, 3-0
Round 5	West Ham United	1-1, 0-2
	1986-87	
Round 3	Manchester City	1-0
Round 4	Coventry City	0-1
	1987-88	
Round 3	Ipswich Town	2-1
Round 4	Chelsea	2-0
Round 5	Arsenal	1-2
	1988-89	
Round 3	Queens Park Rangers	0-0, 2-2, 3-0
Round 4	Oxford United	4-0
Round 5	Bournemouth	1-1, 1-0
Round 6	Nottingham Forest	0-1

Stage	Opponents	Score
1989-90		
Round 3	Nottingham Forest	1-0
Round 4	Hereford United	1-0
Round 5	Newcastle United	3-2
Round 6	Sheffield United	1-0
Semi-Final	Oldham Athletic	3-3, 2-1
Final	Crystal Palace	3-3, 1-0
1990-91		
Round 3	Queens Park Rangers	2-1
Round 4	Bolton Wanderers	1-0
Round 5	Norwich City	1-2
1991-92		
Round 3	Leeds United	1-0
Round 4	Southampton	0-0, 2-2

United lost 2-4 on penalties

Stage	Opponents	Score
1992-93		
Round 3	Bury	2-0
Round 4	Brighton & HA	1-0
Round 5	Sheffield United	1-2
1993-94		
Round 3	Sheffield United	1-0
Round 4	Norwich City	2-0
Round 5	Wimbledon	3-0
Round 6	Charlton Athletic	3-1
Semi-Final	Oldham Athletic	1-1, 4-1
Final	Chelsea	4-0

Stage	Opponents	Score
	1994-95	
Round 3	Sheffield United	2-0
Round 4	Wrexham	5-2
Round 5	Leeds United	3-1
Round 6	Queens Park Rangers	2-0
Semi-Final	Crystal Palace	2-2, 2-0
Final	Everton	0-1
	1995-96	
Round 3	Sunderland	2-2, 2-1
Round 4	Reading	3-0
Round 5	Manchester City	2-1
Round 6	Southampton	2-0
Semi-Final	Chelsea	2-1
Final	Liverpool	1-0
	1996-97	
Round 3	Tottenham Hotspur	2-0
Round 4	Wimbledon	1-1, 0-1

FA Cup Record Club By Club

Opposition	P	W	D	L	F-A
Accrington Stanley	3	2	1	—	14-3
Arsenal	7	3	—	4	9-14
Aston Villa	8	6	—	2	20-11
Barnsley	3	2	1	—	7-2
Birmingham City	9	4	4	1	17-9
Blackburn Rovers	8	2	2	4	12-17
Blackpool	6	4	1	1	16-11
Bolton Wanderers	3	2	—	1	3-3
Bootle Reserves	1	—	—	1	0-1
Bournemouth	6	4	1	1	13-4
Bradford City	2	1	1	—	3-1
Bradford Park Avenue	4	2	2	—	10-2
Brentford	2	1	—	1	7-3
Brighton & HA	6	4	2	—	12-4
Bristol City	1	1	—	—	1-0
Bristol Rovers	3	2	—	1	7-6
Burnley	6	2	1	3	9-17
Burton United	2	1	1	—	4-2
Bury	4	2	1	1	4-2
Cardiff City	1	—	—	1	1-4
Carlisle United	2	1	1	—	5-3
Charlton Athletic	2	2	—	—	5-1
Chelsea	7	6	—	1	14-4
Chester	1	1	—	—	2-1
Colchester United	1	1	—	—	1-0
Coventry City	6	4	1	1	13-6
Crystal Palace	4	2	2	—	8-5
Derby County	8	5	1	2	16-13
Everton	9	4	—	5	6-8
Exeter City	1	1	—	—	3-1
Fleetwood Rovers	1	—	1	—	2-2
Fulham	9	3	4	2	14-12
Grimsby Town	1	—	—	1	0-1
Hartlepool United	1	1	—	—	4-3
Hereford United	1	1	—	—	1-0
Higher Walton	1	1	—	—	2-0
Huddersfield Town	3	2	—	1	8-4
Hull City	2	1	—	1	1-2
Ipswich Town	4	3	—	1	5-2
Kettering Town	2	2	—	—	7-2
Leeds United	9	4	3	2	10-4
Leicester City	2	2	—	—	5-2

Lincoln City	1	—	—	1	1-2
Liverpool	13	7	4	2	21-13
Luton Town	1	1	—	—	2-0
Manchester City	6	4	—	2	11-7
Middlesbrough	9	4	3	2	15-8
Millwall	1	1	—	—	1-0
Nelson	1	1	—	—	3-0
Newcastle United	2	2	—	—	4-2
Northampton Town	1	1	—	—	8-2
Norwich City	5	2	—	3	7-7
Nottingham Forest	6	1	1	4	1-7
Notts County	2	1	1	—	5-4
Oldham Athletic	7	3	3	1	15-9
Oswaldtwistle	1	1	—	—	3-2
Oxford United	2	2	—	—	6-1
Peterborough United	1	1	—	—	3-1
Plymouth Argyle	4	3	—	1	5-4
Port Vale	3	3	—	—	7-2
Portsmouth	7	2	3	2	14-14
Preston North End	9	5	2	2	15-13
Queens Park Rangers	6	4	2	—	10-3
Reading	10	5	4	1	20-9
Rochdale	1	1	—	—	2-0
Rotherham United	2	1	1	—	1-0
Sheffield United	4	3	—	1	5-2
Sheffield Wednesday	9	2	2	5	8-18
South Shore	2	1	—	1	3-3
Southampton	12	6	5	1	21-12
Southport Central	1	1	—	—	4-1
Staple Hill	1	1	—	—	7-2
Stoke City	11	3	5	3	14-13
Sunderland	9	4	5	—	22-13
Swindon Town	2	—	—	2	0-3
Tottenham Hotspur	13	3	5	5	17-21
Walsall	4	2	1	1	4-3
Walthamstow Avenue	2	1	1	—	6-3
Watford	5	3	1	1	6-2
West Bromwich Albion	6	1	3	2	7-11
West Ham United	6	2	1	3	9-10
West Manchester	1	1	—	—	7-0
Weymouth	1	1	—	—	4-0
Wimbledon	3	1	1	1	4-2
Wolves	7	3	2	2	14-11
Workington	1	1	—	—	3-1
Wrexham	2	2	—	—	10-2
Yeovil Town	2	2	—	—	11-0

CREAM OF THE CONTINENT

United's success during the 1990s has given manager Alex Ferguson one of the largest fighting funds in football. With millions at his disposal, Ferguson can trawl the world looking for players that will compliment and subsequently better his team.

Yet the relatively paltry £1.2 million that took Eric Cantona from Elland Road to Old Trafford was one of the best investments he or any other manager has ever made. This purchase, more than any other, turned his team of nearly men into Champions. Cantona went on to make 146 League appearances in United's colours in five seasons, a tally that would undoubtedly have been considerably greater but for his enforced absence following his 'kung-fu kick' at a fan at Selhurst Park.

However, even out of the team Eric's influence on the youngsters around him was considerable; it is no surprise that the club continued picking up honours from all fronts. There were times during his ban when he thought of giving up the game, but Ferguson kept faith with the player, gave him the room to maintain his own fitness regime and gently coaxed him back when the ban was served. That Eric should return and play almost as though he had not been away was a testament to both men's abilities.

Eric's subsequent retirement at the end of the 1996–97 season was not altogether a surprise, for while he is undoubtedly a maverick he is also a totally honest player. If some of his performances during the season were not up to his usual high standard, he would have been the first to say so. And if he could not constantly attain the highest of standards, then it would be in Manchester United and Eric Cantona's best interests if he stepped down. That United have carried on with the same winning formula bears this out.

While much of the attention focused on United in the 1990s has concerned the development and success of the home-grown contingent, Alex Ferguson has not been afraid to spend money overseas when the right players are available. Though he has invested heavily for a series of European hitmen, including Johan Cruyff's son Jordi, who cost £1.4 million from Barcelona, Ole Gunnar Solskjaer (£1.5 million from Molde) and Karel Poborsky (£3.5 million from Slavia Prague), it is goalkeeper Peter Schmeichel whose £550,000 fee from Brondby has been repaid time after time.

Indeed, alongside Cantona, Schmeichel is perhaps the most important foreign capture Ferguson has made. On his day (which is usually most days) there is not a better keeper in the world. Big and strong, fit and agile, he must appear to all intents and purposes as a man mountain to opposing forwards and has often been the difference between picking up one point, when defeat looked on the cards, and three points, when a draw seemed likely. The unbroken success United have enjoyed since Schmeichel's arrival in 1991 has shown Ferguson invested wisely.

THROUGH THE YEARS
APRIL

1908
April
27

Manchester United took part in the first ever FA Charity Shield, drawing 1-1 with QPR (the Southern League Champions) at Stamford Bridge. The match was replayed in August with United winning 4-0.

1915
April
2

United beat Liverpool 2-0 in a League match. Days later a letter appeared in the *Athletic News* asking the authorities to look more closely into the game, which was said to have been the most impassioned in football history; the crowd were booing the players for their lack of effort throughout.

The letter, most probably written by a disgruntled bookmaker (the bookies had taken a rush of bets on United, near the bottom of the First Division, upsetting the form book and beating Liverpool 2-0) did indeed alert the authorities, who questioned just about everyone connected with this match and then, over a year later, announced the result to have been fixed. Life suspensions from the game were handed to virtually every player who took part, although most were lifted immediately after the First World War in recognition of the service given by the players to the war effort. The one exception was Enoch West, who, as well as losing a libel case against the *Athletic News*, did not have his suspension lifted until 1945, when he was 62.

The result was allowed to stand and had repercussions when football resumed – the two points United collected were enough to lift them above Chelsea and out of a relegation spot; when the League was extended immediately after the war, Chelsea were allowed to keep their place because the match had been fixed. Spurs, who would have finished bottom regardless, were voted out in preference to Arsenal, who finished fifth in the Second Division – the only club, therefore, not to have earned their place in the First Division. One other participant in the match was Billy Meredith, who was later to be embroiled in a similar match-rigging claim while playing for Manchester City.

1955

April

2

Duncan Edwards collected the first of 18 caps for England when selected to play against Scotland, a match which England won 7-2. Edwards was England's youngest international player this century at 18 years and 183 days old.

1958

April

19

Bobby Charlton made his first England appearance in the 4-0 win over Scotland at Hampden Park and scored the first of his 49 goals. The same day, Billy Meredith died aged 84.

20 THINGS YOU PROBABLY
NEVER KNEW...

1 In 1958, following the Munich air disaster, UEFA announced that Manchester United would be invited to enter the following season's competition as a gesture of respect, irrespective of where United finished in the League that season. They finally finished the season in eighth place and were duly invited, along with Champions Wolves, into the competition, but both the Football League and the Football Association objected and United did not enter.

2 The Munich air crash so decimated United that they were given special permission to sign and play players for their FA Cup Fifth Round clash with Sheffield Wednesday. Both Ernie Taylor and Stan Crowther were duly signed in time to start the game which was played on 19 February.

3 The closest United have come to hosting a Championship decider was in the last game of the 1951–52 season, when Arsenal visited Old Trafford in second place behind United and needing a 5-0 win in order to take the title from United on goal average. In the event, United won 6-1, a victory so severe it denied Arsenal runners-up spot in the League, which instead went to Spurs!

4 The Premiership clash between United and Liverpool at Old Trafford on 12 October 1996 attracted a crowd of 55,128, the highest seen at all-seater Old Trafford for 12 years.

5 United have since set the record attendance for the Premier League when 55,314 packed in for their clash with Wimbledon on 29 January 1997.

6 United first won the FA Cup in 1909, but in the Fourth Round (equivalent to today's Quarter-Finals) they were 1-0 down to Burnley with 18 minutes remaining when the referee abandoned the game because of snow. United won the replayed game 3-2.

7 In 1949 Matt Busby, four years into his initial five-year contract with United, was offered positions as manager of Spurs and coach of the Italian national side. He turned both down.

8 United's first two home League games of the 1971-72 season were played at Anfield (Liverpool) and the Victoria Ground (Stoke City) as Old Trafford was closed following crowd disturbances the previous season.

9 At the end of the 1985 FA Cup Final Kevin Moran, who had been sent off during the match by referee Peter Willis, was refused permission by the FA to climb the steps at Wembley in order to collect his medal. Indeed, for a while it appeared he would be denied his medal permanently, but following lobbying by the club he was awarded his medal two weeks later.

10 Andrei Kanchelskis became the first player to be sent off in a League Cup Final at Wembley when he was dismissed during the match with Aston Villa in 1994.

11 When Newton Heath went bankrupt in 1902 and a new club was formed, it was initially suggested they should play under the name of either Manchester Celtic or Manchester Central, but the name Manchester United was chosen instead.

12 Their first competitive game as Manchester United was the opening League fixture of the 1902-03 season when they beat Gainsborough Trinity 1-0 in the Second Division.

13 While United's red shirts are world-famous, in 1923 they switched to white shirts with a red V down the front, and white shorts. They reverted to their more traditional colours in 1927.

14 In 1952 Manchester United and Spurs, both of whom were on tour in North America, played exhibition matches in Toronto and New York. Spurs won both, 5-0 and 7-1 respectively, despite the fact United were reigning League Champions!

15 In 1970 United finished third in the FA Cup; the Football Association briefly introduced a play-off match between the two losing Semi-Finalists in order to decide third and fourth places for the competition. United beat Watford 2-0 at Highbury thanks to two goals from Brian Kidd.

16 Gary and Phil Neville are not the only brothers to have won FA Cup medals with United, for the line-up in 1977 against Liverpool included both Brian and Jimmy Greenhoff.

17 Norman Whiteside is the youngest ever FA Cup Final scorer, being 18 years and 18 days when he netted against Brighton in 1983.

18 Whiteside is also the youngest ever League Cup Final scorer, being 17 years and 324 days when he scored against Liverpool that same year. Unfortunately, while United won against Brighton, they'd earlier lost to Liverpool.

19 HP Hardman, who later became chairman of the club, is one of the last amateur players to have won an FA Cup winner's medal, having played for Everton in their 1906 victory.

20 Prior to winning the Double in 1994 United had twice come close to lifting the honour, winning the FA Cup but finishing runners-up in the League in 1948, and winning the League but finishing runners-up in the Cup in 1957.

FOR CLUB AND COUNTRY

There is little in the game that Bobby Charlton has not won – League Championships, the FA Cup, European Cup and over 100 international caps. He is still one of United's favourite sons, and still the most capped player in United's history.

A total of 106 caps puts Sir Bobby third in the list of all-time appearances for England, behind Bobby Moore (108 caps) and Peter Shilton (125). Like Moore (and United team-mate Nobby Stiles), Charlton also holds one of the most sought-after medals in the game; a World Cup winners' medal. Although Bobby did not score in the Final itself, he did register a number of vital goals on the way and still tops the list for having scored more goals for England than anyone else – a total of 49, one ahead of Gary Lineker.

Ever the gentleman, Charlton actually hoped his record would be broken, but no doubt more than a few United fans were not too disappointed when Lineker missed a penalty in a friendly against Brazil that would have equalled the record!

Just behind on United's international roll of honour is Captain Marvel himself, Bryan Robson. His all-action style saw him suffer more than his fair share of injuries, including broken bones, dislocations and assorted pulls and tweaks. Had he avoided even half of those injuries, who knows how many caps he might have eventually won? As it was, he invariably played with little thought for himself, proving an inspirational captain and scoring a healthy 26 goals.

Denis Law won 35 of his 55 Scottish caps while playing for United and finished his career with 30 goals to his credit. This remained the record goalscoring achievement for Scotland until Kenny Dalglish equalled his efforts, although it has to be pointed out that Kenny's 30 goals took him 102 games to achieve while Denis scored as many in just over half that total.

He was an exceptional striker for both club and country; Jimmy Greaves, one of the finest of any era, claims Denis was a better finisher, and he certainly had the ability to score with just about any part of his anatomy. Sadly, as well as missing out on United's finest moment, the 1968 European Cup Final through injury, he never got the opportunity of representing Scotland in the final stages of a major tournament.

While Law was invariably one of the first names on a team sheet for his uncanny ability for scoring goals, then the opposite was true of Martin Buchan, for it was his job to stop them. A high-class defender, he was also an exceptional leader on the field – a quality recognised early on in his career when he was made captain of Aberdeen at the age of 20. He would later become the first man since the Second World War to have skippered winning sides in the FA Cup Final on both sides of the border, leading Aberdeen to victory in 1970 and United in 1977. All but two of his caps were earned while playing for United, and his influence at the heart of the United defence was missed for a number of years following his transfer to Oldham at the start of the 1983-84 season.

It is not often Alex Ferguson makes a mistake, but the decision to allow Mark Hughes to join Chelsea in July 1995 must be one. Certainly, a year later Alex was honest enough to admit he might have been a little hasty in allowing Mark to move on, for one of the most feared strikers in the modern game had lost none of his appetite, ability or goalscoring prowess. If there is a better player at shielding the ball, waiting for team-mates to come up in support and then lay off a telling pass, then he has yet to be found.

Hughes's role within the sides he has played for has often meant he has received a fair few kicks and knocks during the course of 90 minutes, but he is also more than capable of taking care of himself and giving defenders one or two knocks back. He has proven just as vital to the national cause, hitting 16 goals since his first cap in 1984. As with many of his ilk, it remains a major pity he has not been able to grace the World Cup or European Championship Finals during his career.

Fellow Welshman Clayton Blackmore was something of an unsung hero during his time with Manchester United, working quietly yet effectively in midfield or on either flank. If the fans were not always sure of what he had contributed then his fellow professionals were seldom in any doubt, for Clayton was one of the most reliable players within any side. He followed former United player Bryan Robson to Middlesbrough in 1994 and after a brief spell on loan with Bristol City, returned to the Middlesbrough line-up and played perhaps the best football of his career, earning a recall to the Welsh line-up to claim his 39th cap.

Ryan Giggs currently lies fourth in the list of top Welsh internationals on United's books, but there is no doubt he will continue to climb over the next few years as he remains as important to the national side as he does to the Red Devils.

Sammy McIlroy was first spotted by Matt Busby while a 15-year-old, but showed enough promise for United to offer him a contract in September 1969, turning professional two years later. He made his first appearance during the 1971-72 season (scoring on his debut against Manchester City) and spent ten seasons with the club, winning an FA Cup winner's and Second Division Championship medal as well as suffering the despair of relegation. First capped for Northern Ireland in 1972, he went on to win a total of 88 caps, 52 of these being earned while a United player. In 1982 he moved on to Stoke City, but after relegation from the First Division in 1985 returned to Manchester, this time signing with City.

Jimmy Nicholl's United career was seemingly brief, for he made his debut for the club during the 1974-75 season and left shortly after the start of the 1981-82 campaign, but in that short space of time established himself as a good quality full-back for both club and country. While he lost his club place to John Gidman and subsequently joined Sunderland, he was an integral part of the Northern Ireland side that reached the World Cup Finals of both 1982 and 1986.

Of course, the player who should be at the top of this list is George Best, one of the greatest footballing talents the game has ever produced. United fans fortunate enough to have seen him during his heyday will confirm him as a two-footed, quick-witted genius who could both make and score goals, though often a second ball, so that the other 21 players on the pitch had something to do, would not have gone amiss! As it was, the retirement of Sir Matt Busby seemed to send George's career into decline, with disciplinary problems and disappearances getting more headlines and coverage than his efforts on the field.

Denis Irwin's consistently high quality displays in a United shirt make a mockery of what he cost the club when switching from Oldham Athletic in 1990 – the highly experienced defender has repaid the £625,000 fee time and time again. He began his career with Leeds United but after 72 League games was given a free transfer, a deal which now seems little more than absurd. Since arriving at United he has become a regular fixture within the Eire side, collecting 45 caps, and has won four Premiership titles, two FA Cups, the League Cup, a European Cup Winners' Cup and three Charity Shields. Add to this his ability as a free-kick specialist and you can appreciate his true worth.

Kevin Moran is assured his place in football history, but unfortunately it is a record he would rather forget; in 1985, playing for United against Everton at Wembley, he became the first player to be sent off during an FA Cup Final.

WORST SEASON 1

**Although United had finished the previous
season in 17th place in the First Division,
there were those who reckoned they might
be a good outside bet for the title in
1930–31. Manager Herbert Bamlett
had enjoyed three years in which to fashion
the side and, if he was to make an
impact at the club, then this was the
season to do it.**

History tells its own story of the season, for everything
that could have gone wrong did; United lost their
opening 12 League games, a Football League record.
These were not narrow single-goal defeats, either, for West
Ham scored five, Chelsea and Huddersfield rattled six and
Newcastle hit seven (at Old Trafford) during that opening
spell.

By the time United secured their first points with a 2–0
home win over Birmingham City, they were as good as
doomed – and November had barely started. Even this
victory was a temporary respite, for three defeats and two
draws in the next five games left United with only four points
from their first 18 games!

While relegation was now a near-certainty, United could
still muster some pride and try to salvage something from a
season which had started with high expectations. Despite
registering only seven victories all season, including only one
away from home (at Sunderland 2–1), they did manage to win

4-1 on two occasions, against Sheffield Wednesday and Liverpool.

But really the sorry story was United's defence porous defence, which shipped in 115 goals; aside from the early-season batterings, Aston Villa also hit seven and Derby got six. Before the end of the season, with the cause a lost and hopeless one, manager Bamlett resigned. By the time the season ended, United were bottom of the First Division with 22 points, nine adrift of the next club Leeds United.

1930-31 LEAGUE RECORD

Opponents	Home	Away
Arsenal	1-2	1-4
Aston Villa	3-4	0-7
Birmingham	2-0	0-0
Blackburn Rovers	0-1	1-4
Blackpool	0-0	1-5
Bolton Wanderers	1-1	1-3
Chelsea	1-0	2-6
Derby County	2-1	1-6
Grimsby Town	0-2	1-2
Huddersfield Town	0-6	0-3
Leeds United	0-0	0-5
Leicester City	0-0	4-5
Liverpool	4-1	1-1
Manchester City	1-3	1-4
Middlesbrough	4-4	1-3
Portsmouth	0-1	1-4
Newcastle United	4-7	3-4
Sheffield United	1-2	1-3
Sheffield Wednesday	4-1	0-3
Sunderland	1-1	2-1
West Ham United	1-0	1-5

DOUBLE ACTS

Changes in formation and the way the game is played have, over the years, given rise to a new phenomenon; that of double acts.

The old days of a 2-3-5 line-up invariably meant there had to be almost telepathic understanding between various members of the team; the full-back had to know what his immediate half-back was likely to do, while he in turn would need to keep the winger fed. It was perhaps only the two full-backs who ever got a chance to develop into a double act we would recognise and understand today, not least because as well as the last line of defence (barring the goalkeeper), they were the first line of attack.

In recent years it has been the central defensive duo that has needed to develop the best understanding, not least because any decision to move up in an attempt to catch the opposing team offside will be taken by either of these two players. The United side of recent years had not one but two good double acts; Steve Bruce and Gary Pallister operating in central defence, and the brothers Phil and Gary Neville playing in the full-back positions. That the two brothers should have an understanding goes without saying, for they had spent many of their formative years honing their skills with each other, knocking the ball from one to the other and laying the foundations that served both well when they broke into the

United first team. That they should then have gone on to repeat their partnership for England says much for their talents.

There are many who felt that Bruce and Pallister should have been given the opportunity of repeating their partnership for England, for there is little doubt their solid style made United such a difficult side to break down at club level. In the event, only Gary was picked with any regularity for the national side.

Another vital partnership is to be found in the front line. The great United side of the 1960s contained a potent mixture, with George Best, Bobby Charlton and Denis Law always likely to pop up and score from almost any angle, but at no point could you have said that any two of the three were operating as a partnership. The two most likely to have done so, Law and Charlton, were invariably at the mercy of George Best in supplying the final pass, a pass that would arrive infrequently as George often tried for a goal himself.

Alex Ferguson has long recognised the need for an effective partnership, linking Mark Hughes of Wales with Brian McClair of Scotland in the first great United side he assembled. It was perhaps Hughes who had the most important role within the pairing, for his ability to hold the ball up, take any amount of batterings from defenders and lay the ball off effectively took a lot of the pressure off McClair, enabling him to get into a scoring position.

Not that McClair's contribution should be underestimated. The man Alex Ferguson called 'a model professional' scored the winning goal in the 1992 League Cup Final, and he also notched two years later at Wembley in the FA Cup. While also used in a more withdrawn role, he scored 24 in his first season at Old Trafford as an out and out striker – the first player to top 20 goals since George Best in 1968.

When Mark was sold to Chelsea and Eric Cantona and Andy Cole introduced to the side, there were many who thought this new pairing would prove irresistible, but the reality was different. Andy had arrived from a side that played to his strengths, running on to through balls delivered by fellow strikers and midfield players alike. At United, he found the going difficult at first, not least because of Eric's maverick nature.

It is noticeable that Cantona's retirement and the introduction of Teddy Sheringham has had a beneficial effect on Andy's fortunes, with goals coming at the same kind of rate at which he was grabbing them for Newcastle. The credit for this must go to Teddy, for what he lacks in pace he more than makes up for with intelligence; an intelligence to read the game exceptionally well, knowing when to lay the ball off short, when to hit it long, making runs into space that take defenders away from the danger area, knowing Cole will be filling that space and scoring.

Indeed, so successful has the partnership been at club level that there have been growing demands for the pair to link up for England, not least because of the enforced absence of Alan Shearer and the drying up of goals for Ian Wright. Playing alongside Teddy has enabled Andy to develop another side to his game that had not previously been seen, for he too has learned that the game remains a team game, and passing ability is a skill just as vital as scoring. All this makes United an even more potent force than previously!

THROUGH THE YEARS
MAY

1968
May
29

United became the first English side to win the European Cup with a 4-1 extra time twin over Benfica thanks to goals from Bobby Charlton (two), George Best and birthday boy Brian Kidd.

1991
May
15

United made it a triumphant return for English clubs in European competition with a 2-1 win over Barcelona in the Cup Winners' Cup. Mark Hughes grabbed both United's goals, the perfect pay off following his unhappy spell at Barcelona.

1993
May
2

Alex Ferguson becomes the first manager to lead sides to the Championship in both Scotland (with Aberdeen) and England (with Manchester United), courtesy of Oldham Athletic's 1–0 win at Aston Villa. It was United's first title since 1967.

1967
May
6

'My finest hour' was Matt Busby's verdict as Manchester United came away from West Ham's cramped Boleyn Ground with a 6–1 win – and their seventh Championship – under their belt. They'd clinched the title from nearest challengers Forest and Spurs with a match to spare.

1942
May
18

Today saw the toothless arrival of Norbert P Stiles in Salford, Manchester. A United stalwart from 1960 to 1971, he's been immortalised in 'Three Lions' as 'Nobby dancing', a reference to his (also toothless) victory jig at Wembley with the World Cup in 1966.

GREAT MIDFIELDERS

The engine room of every Old Trafford team has been crucial to the successes achieved. We look here at some of the most inspirational operators in the middle of the park.

 ## DUNCAN EDWARDS

There is no telling just how much Duncan Edwards might have achieved in the game had it not been for the Munich air disaster. He was already a great player – the youngest man this century to have been picked for England, an inspirational figure for club and country, an exceptional footballing talent and a quiet and modest man.

Born in Dudley on 1 October 1936, he signed with United as an amateur after much persuading by both Jimmy Murphy and Matt Busby. He was a regular in the side that won the first three FA Youth Cups, but had also broken into the first team as well, making his debut in April 1953 in the 4-1 defeat by Cardiff. The following season his appearances began to grow, and the maturity he displayed on the pitch belied his youth.

In April 1955 he was handed the first of his 18 full caps for England, at the age 18 years and 183 days, and there can be no doubt that but for Munich he would have gone on to register well over 100 appearances in an England shirt. Aside from this he won two League titles with United and was a member of the side which were runners-up in the FA Cup in 1957.

Such was his physical and mental strength that, despite the horrific injuries sustained in the air crash, he kept battling for life for almost two weeks. It is said that the death of Edwards affected Busby most (although he would surely have been equally devastated by the loss of each and every one of the players who died), but it would perhaps be nearly the truth to say that he was never able to replace Duncan in his team – no one could.

The proud town of Dudley erected a permanent memorial to their most famous son; a stained glass window in the church in the town that tells the story of this most unique of footballers.

DUNCAN EDWARDS UNITED RECORD 1953-58									
League		**FA Cup**		**League Cup**		**Europe**		**Total**	
Apps	Goals	Apps	Goals	Apps	Goals	Apps	Goals	Apps	Goals
151	20	12	1	—	—	12	—	175	21

BRYAN ROBSON

There are many superlatives used when describing Bryan Robson, and he is entitled to all of them, for few players have shown as much commitment to the cause for both club and country. When the odds seemed stacked against United or England, the goals wouldn't come or something inspirational was needed to wrest a point out of defeat, Bryan could usually be relied upon to do the job.

Born in Witton Gilbert on 11 January 1957, he joined West Bromwich Albion as an apprentice in 1974 and quickly established himself in the first team, making over 200 appearances for the Baggies before former West Brom manager Ron Atkinson, having moved on to Old Trafford, targetted Bryan as the man he most wanted in his team. A British record transfer of £1.5 million secured Bryan's signature in 1981 and he was soon the engine room of the midfield and captain of the side.

Under Atkinson, Robson had the honour of leading United to two FA Cup wins (in 1983 and 1985), and the subsequent arrival of Alex Ferguson brought more Cup glory with a further FA Cup in 1990 and the following season's European Cup Winners' Cup. By the time Alex Ferguson had assembled the side that would finally bring the title back to Old Trafford, Bryan had been effectively replaced as captain by Steve Bruce, but still had a vital part to play in helping United win two League titles.

He was left out of the side which made it a Double celebration, not even getting a place on the substitutes' bench, a decision which upset Robson but which showed the mettle of both men involved – Ferguson would not give in to sentiment, picking a side to win the game irrespective of whether it meant leaving out Robson, the player feeling he still had much to offer.

At the end of the 1993–94 season he was given a free transfer and promptly became player-manager of Middlesbrough, taking his side to the First Division title in his first season. Although the club were relegated at the end of the 1996–97 campaign, they did reach the Finals of both the FA Cup and League Cup and in 1998 were bidding for a swift return.

BRYAN ROBSON UNITED RECORD 1981-94									
League		FA Cup		League Cup		Europe		Total	
Apps	Goals	Apps	Goals	Apps	Goals	Apps	Goals	Apps	Goals
345	74	35	10	51	5	32	11	463	100

ERIC CANTONA

Eric Cantona's premature decision to retire at the end of the 1996–97 season robbed the game of one of its characters. He arrived in England in 1991 with a reputation for being a fiery individual, quick to criticise team mates and management alike, a player who most of his managers in France had found difficult to handle. He left England in 1997 with a clutch of medals, accolades and the hero-worship of thousands.

Born in Nimes on 24 May 1966 he played for numerous clubs in France, usually falling foul of the management, before arriving in England. Leeds paid £900,000 for his signature, and during his first season he helped the club win the First Division Championship, breaking United hearts into the bargain as they finished runners-up. In November of the following season he was surprisingly let go, Alex Ferguson paying £1.2 million to bring him to Old Trafford.

It was the introduction of Eric that turned United from contenders into title-winners by the season's end, as United finally ended their long barren spell. He helped them retain the title the following season, becoming the first man to win three consecutive title medals with more than one club.

In January 1995 he was involved in a fracas with a spectator at Selhurst Park and earned a seven-month ban from the game. This probably cost United their chance of making it three titles on the trot, but he returned midway through the following season to resume where he had left off, guiding United to two further titles.

He also played in both the FA Cup Finals that enabled them to win the Double, scoring twice in the first game against Chelsea and getting the vital strike against Liverpool. He was capped 45 times by France, a figure that should have been considerably higher had his outspoken nature not counted against him. A refreshingly honest man, he decided to retire from the game he had graced rather than accept a dip in his own high playing standards.

ERIC CANTONA UNITED RECORD 1992-97									
League		FA Cup		League Cup		Europe		Total	
Apps	Goals	Apps	Goals	Apps	Goals	Apps	Goals	Apps	Goals
143	64	17	10	6	1	19	7	185	82

 # ROY KEANE

The transfer of Paul Ince to Internazionale of Milan and the retirement of Eric Cantona would, on the face of it, appear to have decimated the United midfield, but the emergence of Roy Keane – as a man with the spirit and tough tackling of both Bryan Robson and Paul Ince, the passing ability of Ray Wilkins and the inspirational qualities of Eric Cantona – has done much to soften the blow.

First discovered playing in Ireland for Cobh Ramblers, he was recommended to Nottingham Forest and signed for £10,000 in 1990. Although initially homesick, Keane's performances in the side culminated with an appearance at Wembley in the FA Cup Final at the end of his first season, although Forest were beaten 2-1 by Spurs.

With Forest suffering relegation at the end of the first season of the Premier League, it was obvious Roy Keane would not be happy playing First Division football, a situation that alerted several managers as to a possible transfer. In the end Alex Ferguson secured his services in return for a £3.75 million fee and Roy quickly slotted into the United midfield.

In the four years since, he has collected three League titles, two FA Cups and two Charity Shields, as well as continued interest from overseas, most of whose top clubs would be happy to land the inspirational Republic of Ireland player. At the end of the 1995-96 season Bobby Robson of Barcelona made discreet enquiries to try and land the player, but Keane subsequently signed a new four-year contract with United.

Like his predecessor Bryan Robson, his robust playing style has seen him suffer more than his fair share of injuries – but, also like Robson, he invariably bounces back better than ever.

ROY KEANE UNITED RECORD 1993-(97)									
League		FA Cup		League Cup		Europe		Total	
Apps	Goals	Apps	Goals	Apps	Goals	Apps	Goals	Apps	Goals
112	15	23	1	11	—	17	4	163	20

PLAYER TALK

Footballers have brains in their boots – but these Old Trafford favourites chose to put their thoughts into words

'I hate losing. It stinks.'

*Peter Schmeichel after FA Cup Final
defeat against Everton, 1995*

'It's an overwhelming and inspiring place, Old Trafford, like being in a palace. It came as a culture shock – even the loos have gold taps!'

Garry Birtles

'All I could see was the ball. I thought I had a 50-50 chance of getting it.'

Kevin Moran on his Wembley sending-off, 1985

'Manchester United offered me a really excellent contract, but what City offered was far in excess – I couldn't believe it, it was much too high.'

*Trevor Francis on why he made the wrong choice
of Manchester club*

'I'm only just good enough for United – if I go to Italy it will only be for a holiday,'

Roy Keane quashes transfer speculation in modest style.

'I don't know if I've got a footballing brain. I only got one O-Level at school, but that *was* in PE.'

Teddy Sheringham

'My ambition is to stay with United until the end of my playing career.'   *Brian McClair*

'I am a confident person – I never doubt my own ability.'
David Beckham

'I went up to him afterwards, shook his hand and called him a bastard.'
Wimbledon keeper Neil Sullivan after Beckham's wondergoal

'A dustbin could have kept goal for us in some games, the defence has been so good.'
Peter Schmeichel in the aftermath of his first title

'I'd be worth around £14 to £15 million by today's prices.'
George Best, 1996

'I would not change anything, nothing at all. I am not always pleased with myself, but that's the way I am.'   *Eric Cantona*

'If you need motivating to play for Manchester United, then you shouldn't be at the club.'   *Gary Neville*

'If we played the team of '68 we'd beat them 10-0.'
Peter Schmeichel

'It's very difficult to compare the teams. the gap is so great time-wise, but there are certainly similarities within the team. They have that right blend of experience, youth and world-class players – just like we had.'
Team of '68 veteran Denis Law

'Everybody wishes they could play forever, but they can't.'
Sir Bobby Charlton

THROUGH THE YEARS
JUNE

1982
June
17

In the World Cup held in Spain, Norman Whiteside, who had made just two League appearances for United, became the youngest player to compete in the final stages when he played for Northern Ireland against Yugoslavia. He was just 17 years and 41 days old.

The talented Whiteside played over 200 League games for United but less than 30 with Everton, to whom he was transferred in 1989. Injury forced his retirement at the age of just 25.

1969
June
10

Central defender Ronny Johnsen was born in Sandefjord, Norway. By the time he reached Old Trafford in 1996, he'd played for Eik, Lyn and Lillestrom in his home country, as well as Besiktas in Turkey where he clocked up a season's worth of appearances.

1966
June
29

A United double act tore Norway apart – with a little help from four-goal Jimmy Greaves – as England won 6-1 in the Ullevaal Stadium. Bobby Charlton had one of his best games in an England shirt, laying on the sixth goal for the also impressive John Connelly by nutmegging a hapless home defender.

It all set up the team nicely for the World Cup Finals the following month. Though Connelly was not to play a major part, appearing only in the first game against Uruguay before giving way to Martin Peters, Bobby Charlton set them on their way to the trophy with a classic goal against Mexico.

1988
June
12

Central defender Kevin Moran and Paul McGrath faced club-mate and captain Bryan Robson as the Republic of Ireland took England down a peg or two in the European Championship Finals in Germany. Neil Webb, then of Nottingham Forest but soon to be a Red, was also one of the embarrassed men in white shirts.

GREAT MATCHES

United's history has been studded with sporting challenges – most of which they've risen to with Championship class. Here are just a few of these memorable matches.

**Millwall 0 Manchester United 2
5 May 1934
League Division Two**

Outside Cup Finals and League Championship deciders, of which there have been many, the most important match (as opposed to one of their best games) during United's long and illustrious history was undoubtedly the closing game of the 1933-34 season. United had struggled and by the last game of the season were occupying the second relegation spot. Lincoln, in bottom place, were already down, so the final place was between United, Swansea and, irony upon irony, Millwall. Defeat or a draw would see United relegated to the Third Division for the first time in their history, and they were facing a Millwall side that were renowned fighters at their own Den ground.

The opening minutes saw Millwall tear into their opponents, but United's defence held firm and the Reds began to get a grip on the game, allowing the wing pairing of Manley and Cape to gain control. Indeed, it was Manley who both began and finished the move that led to United's opening goal after eight minutes, sending Cape away along the wing and racing into the box to net the return. And, as important as that first goal was, there was still the need to prevent Millwall from equalising. Two minutes into the second half Cape extended the lead with a powerful shot, and although that ended the scoring there were still plenty of heart-stopping moments before United could emerge triumphant, sending Millwall into the Third Division as a result.

It is of course entirely hypothetical, but relegation to the Third Division could have been catastrophic for United; the subsequent domination of the game of the 1950s might never have happened, the quest for the European Cup a fanciful dream and their re-emergence in the 1990s unlikely. Relegation might well have left Manchester United on a par with the likes of current fallen giants Preston, Huddersfield and Burnley.

Team: Hacking, Griffiths, Jones, Robertson, Vose, McKay, Cape, McLenahan, Ball, Hine, Manley.

Arsenal 4 Manchester United 5
1 February 1958
League Division One

It was not apparent at the time, but this match was the last played on British soil by perhaps the greatest side to have represented United in their history. And while their opponents, Arsenal, were not the force of old and still in a transition period that would last a further 12 years, there was still something magical about the arrival of Manchester United in London that drew huge crowds wherever they played.

United arrived at Highbury as reigning League Champions, having won the title for the previous two seasons. They were also leading the charge and looking likely to lift a third consecutive title for only the third time in the League's history (Huddersfield in the 1920s and Arsenal themselves in the 1930s having previously achieved the feat). And in the first half United played as Champions, opening up a seemingly unassailable 3-0 lead through Duncan Edwards, Tommy Taylor and Bobby Charlton. Conversation at half time centred on how many United might win by; not only were they head and shoulders above Arsenal but they were taking the game to new heights.

After a blank opening 15 minutes of the second half, Arsenal began to grow in confidence, and after David Herd had put the home side back in the game, two goals in quick succession from Bloomfield put the sides level.

United appeared on the ropes, but Edwards in particular took the game by the scruff of the neck, Viollet, and then Taylor, with his second, put United back in charge. Even that was not the end of matters, for a goal from Tapscott reduced the lead to one goal and set up a final frantic charge by Arsenal.

When the final whistle went there was relief from United, disappointment from Arsenal and appreciation from both sets of supporters for a truly remarkable game. Little did they know as they made their way home that in just under a week's time the great United side they had just witnessed would be no more.

Team: Gregg, Foulkes, Byrne, Colman, Jones, Edwards, Morgan, Charlton, Taylor, Viollet, Scanlon.

Manchester United 4 Benfica 1
29 May 1968
European Cup Final

Although United had at last managed to make the European Cup Final after three previous Semi-Final disappointments, only winning the trophy would provide the perfect memorial to those who had perished in the Munich disaster some ten years previously. Only winning the trophy would satisfy manager Matt Busby, his team and the hordes of United's followers who swamped Wembley for the Final.

Standing in their way were equally seasoned European Cup campaigners Benfica, with several of the hugely successful Portuguese national side in their line-up, including the incomparable Eusebio, Torres and Simoes. The first half was uninspiring, both teams tentatively probing and testing without ever seriously threatening either goal.

The tempo picked up in the second half, as expected given what was at stake, and United made the first breakthrough when Bobby Charlton netted a glancing header from Sadler's cross. As the game wore on, that goal looked enough to have won the trophy, but with barely ten minutes left Graca hit an equaliser that deflated United for a vital five minutes.

Indeed, Eusebio might have scored a winner with only four minutes left on the clock but, in wanting to score the perfect goal rather than a simple tap-in, allowed a chance to go begging.

Having been given a reprieve, United set about their business, at last, in extra time, netting three goals from George Best, Brian Kidd (celebrating his 19th birthday) and a second from Charlton.

When the final whistle blew and United's ultimate dream became reality, there were two abiding memories of the game that will forever live in the memory. The first was that during the heat of the battle Eusebio, perhaps one of the finest sportsmen to have graced the game, took time out from his labours to shake Alex Stepney's hand in recognition of a fine save.

The second, and probably most emotional, was the scene at the very end when Matt Busby, Bobby Charlton and Bill Foulkes, three survivors from the Munich disaster, embraced each other in joyful celebration.

Team: Stepney, Brennan, Dunne, Crerand, Foulkes, Stiles, Best, Kidd, Charlton, Sadler, Aston.

Manchester United 3 Blackburn Rovers 1
3 May 1993
FA Premier League

There have been many better games, more resounding wins and perhaps even more important games than this end-of-season clash, but since this was the game that confirmed United as Champions, after a wait of some 26 years, it will live long in the memory of their followers.

In truth, of course, the title was already won; Oldham's surprise 1-0 win at Villa Park 24 hours previously had removed the final obstacle for United. But manager Alex Ferguson was keen to serve notice that United intended dominating English club football for the rest of the decade and that nothing less than victory in the final two games of the season would be good enough. There were plenty of sore heads among the United faithful when their team took to the field on this occasion, and judging by their first half performance, perhaps even one or two among the players, for Blackburn were showing they had every intention of gatecrashing the party.

In the end, goals from Ryan Giggs, Paul Ince and Gary Pallister (his first of the season) gave United a deserved victory. Blackburn's role in the event may have been a supporting one, but two years on they took centre stage, pushing United into second place. That was still in the future, however, for after receiving the trophy United's party began in earnest.

Team: Schmeichel, Parker, Irwin, Blackmore, Pallister, Ince, McClair (Kanchelskis), Hughes, Sharpe (Robson) Giggs, Cantona.

Manchester United 4 Chelsea 0
14 May 1994
FA Cup Final

After early Double successes by Preston and Aston Villa, the football world had to wait over 60 years for the feat to be done again, with Spurs finally achieving the dream in 1961. Ten years later Arsenal won the Double, followed a further 15 years later by Liverpool. Having finally proved capable of winning the title in the 1990s, United's followers now demanded a twin assault on the European Cup and the domestic Double.

Having secured the title in 1994, attention could now turn to the other half of the domestic dream. Luck seemed to be on their side as they survived a scare in the Semi-Final before overcoming Oldham after a replay. Even so, while they were acknowledged as the best side in the country, they faced a resurgent Chelsea team who had proven to be something of a bogey side in recent years. Indeed, United's first two defeats during the season had both been inflicted by Chelsea!

On Wembley's lush and spacious turf, both teams began hesitantly, not wishing to give too much away to their opponents. If anything Chelsea, whose search for a major trophy stretched over 20 years, had the better of the opening half. Slowly but surely, however, United got the better of Chelsea and finally took the lead on the hour thanks to an Eric Cantona penalty. He added another dubious penalty seven minutes later, and the fight seemed to drain from Chelsea. The final score of 4-0 (Hughes and McClair added later goals) may have flattered United, but few would deny they thoroughly deserved to complete the Double. Two years later they became the first side to do the Double for a second time and fully justify their tag of 'team of the 1990s'.

Team: Schmeichel, Parker, Irwin (Sharpe), Bruce, Kanchelskis (McClair), Pallister, Cantona, Ince, Keane, Hughes, Giggs.

LEAGUE CUP RECORD

Just one win in four Finals for United in English football's youngest Cup competition – here are the full statistics.

Stage	Opponents	Score
1960-61		
Round 1	Exeter City	1-1, 4-1
Round 2	Bradford City	1-2
1961-62		
Did not enter		
1962-63		
Did not enter		
1963-64		
Did not enter		
1964-65		
Did not enter		
1965-66		
Did not enter		
1966-67		
Did not enter		

Stage	Opponents	Score
	1967-68	
	Did not enter	
	1968-69	
	Did not enter	
	1969-70	
Round 2	Middlesbrough	1-0
Round 3	Wrexham	2-0
Round 4	Burnley	0-0, 1-0
Round 5	Derby County	0-0, 1-0
Semi-Final	Manchester City	1-2, 2-2
	1970-71	
Round 2	Aldershot	3-1
Round 3	Portsmouth	1-0
Round 4	Chelsea	2-1
Round 5	Crystal Palace	4-2
Semi-Final	Aston Villa	1-1, 1-2
	1971-72	
Round 2	Ipswich Town	3-1
Round 3	Burnley	1-1, 1-0
Round 4	Stoke City	1-1, 0-0, 1-2
	1972-73	
Round 2	Oxford United	2-2, 3-1
Round 3	Bristol Rovers	1-1, 1-2
	1973-74	
Round 2	Middlesbrough	0-1

Stage	Opponents	Score
1974-75		
Round 2	Charlton Athletic	5-1
Round 3	Manchester City	1-0
Round 4	Burnley	3-2
Round 5	Middlesbrough	0-0, 3-0
Semi-Final	Norwich City	2-2, 0-1
1975-76		
Round 2	Brentford	2-1
Round 3	Aston Villa	2-1
Round 4	Manchester City	0-4
1976-77		
Round 2	Tranmere Rovers	5-0
Round 3	Sunderland	2-2, 2-2, 1-0
Round 4	Newcastle United	7-2
Round 5	Everton	0-3
1977-78		
Round 2	Arsenal	2-3
1978-79		
Round 2	Stockport County	3-2
Round 3	Watford	1-2
1979-80		
Round 2	Tottenham Hotspur	1-2, 3-1
Round 3	Norwich City	1-4
1980-81		
Round 2	Coventry City	0-1, 0-1

Stage	Opponents	Score
	1981-82	
Round 2	Tottenham Hotspur	0-1, 0-1
	1982-83	
Round 2	Bournemouth	2-0, 2-2
Round 3	Bradford City	0-0, 4-1
Round 4	Southampton	2-0
Round 5	Nottingham Forest	4-0
Semi-Final	Arsenal	4-2, 2-1
Final	Liverpool	1-2
	1983-84	
Round 2	Port Vale	1-0, 2-0
Round 3	Colchester United	2-0
Round 4	Oxford United	1-1, 1-1, 1-2
	1984-85	
Round 2	Burnley	4-0, 3-0
Round 3	Everton	1-2
	1985-86	
Round 2	Crystal Palace	1-0, 1-0
Round 3	West Ham United	1-0
Round 4	Liverpool	1-2
	1986-87	
Round 2	Port Vale	2-0, 5-2
Round 3	Southampton	0-0, 1-4

Stage	Opponents	Score
1987-88		
Round 2	Hull City	5-0, 1-0
Round 3	Crystal Palace	2-1
Round 4	Bury	2-1
Round 5	Oxford United	0-2
1988-89		
Round 2	Rotherham United	1-0, 5-0
Round 3	Wimbledon	1-2
1989-90		
Round 2	Portsmouth	3-2, 0-0
Round 3	Tottenham Hotspur	0-3
1990-91		
Round 2	Halifax Town	3-1, 2-1
Round 3	Liverpool	3-1
Round 4	Arsenal	6-2
Round 5	Southampton	1-1, 3-2
Semi-Final	Leeds United	2-1, 1-0
Final	Sheffield Wednesday	0-1
1991-92		
Round 2	Cambridge United	3-0, 1-1
Round 3	Portsmouth	3-1
Round 4	Oldham Athletic	2-0
Round 5	Leeds United	3-1
Semi-Final	Middlesbrough	0-0, 2-1
Final	Nottingham Forest	1-0
1992-93		
Round 2	Brighton & HA	1-1, 1-0
Round 3	Aston Villa	0-1

Stage	Opponents	Score
	1993-94	
Round 2	Stoke City	1-2, 2-0
Round 3	Leicester City	5-1
Round 4	Everton	2-0
Round 5	Portsmouth	2-2, 1-0
Semi-Final	Sheffield Wednesday	1-0, 4-1
Final	Aston Villa	1-3
	1994-95	
Round 2	Port Vale	2-1, 2-0
Round 3	Newcastle United	0-2
	1995-96	
Round 2	York City	0-3, 3-1
	1996-97	
Round 3	Swindon Town	2-1
Round 4	Leicester City	0-2
	1997-98	
Round 3	Ipswich Town	0-2

League Cup Record Club By Club

Opposition	P	W	D	L	F-A
Aldershot	1	1	—	—	3-1
Arsenal	4	3	—	1	14-8
Aston Villa	5	1	1	3	5-8
Bournemouth	2	1	1	—	4-2
Bradford City	3	1	1	1	5-3
Brentford	1	1	—	—	2-1
Brighton & HA	2	1	1	—	2-1
Bristol Rovers	2	—	1	1	2-3
Burnley	7	5	2	—	13-3
Bury	1	1	—	—	2-1
Cambridge United	2	1	1	—	4-1
Charlton Athletic	1	1	—	—	5-1
Chelsea	1	1	—	—	2-1
Colchester United	1	1	—	—	2-0
Coventry City	2	—	—	2	0-2
Crystal Palace	4	4	—	—	8-3
Derby County	2	1	1	—	1-0
Everton	3	1	—	2	3-5
Exeter City	2	1	1	—	5-2
Halifax Town	2	2	—	—	5-2
Hull City	2	2	—	—	6-0
Ipswich Town	2	1	—	1	3-3

Opposition	P	W	D	L	F-A
Leeds United	3	3	—	—	6-2
Leicester City	2	1	—	1	5-3
Liverpool	3	1	—	2	5-5
Manchester City	4	1	1	2	4-8
Middlesbrough	6	3	2	1	6-2
Newcastle United	2	1	—	1	7-4
Norwich City	3	—	1	2	3-7
Nottingham Forest	2	2	—	—	5-0
Oldham Athletic	1	1	—	—	2-0
Oxford United	6	1	3	2	8-9
Port Vale	6	6	—	—	14-3
Portsmouth	6	4	2	—	10-5
Rotherham United	2	2	—	—	6-0
Sheffield Wednesday	3	2	—	1	5-2
Southampton	5	2	2	1	3-4
Stockport County	1	1	—	—	7-5
Stoke City	5	1	2	2	5-5
Sunderland	3	1	2	—	5-4
Swindon Town	1	1	—	—	2-1
Tottenham Hotspur	5	1	—	4	4-8
Tranmere Rovers	1	1	—	—	5-0
Watford	1	—	—	1	1-2
West Ham United	1	1	—	—	1-0
Wimbledon	1	—	—	1	1-2
Wrexham	1	1	—	—	2-0
York City	2	1	—	1	3-4

THE  FILES

The Manchester United manager's job is the most sought-after in football. We profile the men who've met that challenge over the years with ratings out of five.

Ernest Mangnall
1903–12
Honours: Division One Champions   1907–08, 1910–11
         FA Cup winners   1908–09

When James West resigned as secretary in 1903, the United directors moved swiftly to appoint his counterpart at Burnley, Ernest Mangnall. Having combined the roles of secretary and manager at Turf Moor, he assumed both posts at United. He has since become known as the Matt Busby of his era, being able to motivate players, spot raw talent and possessing a thirst for success unmatched at United until Busby and, later, Ferguson walked through the doors.

He was also not afraid to take on players other clubs found trouble; when an illegal betting scandal engulfed Manchester City, Mangnall swooped to sign four of the players who were suspended! With this quartet in place, Mangnall fashioned a side that brought the League title to Old Trafford for the first time in United's history, later adding another title and the FA Cup during his reign. He resigned in 1912 and went on to manage…Manchester City!

John Robson
1914–21
Honours: None

John Robson's place in history is assured, for he was the first United official to hold the title of manager. Although Mangnall had certainly carried out managerial duties, his official title was that of secretary. Robson officially took over as manager in 1914 and two years later, following the resignation of J Bentley, also assumed secretarial duties, although the First World War was severely curtailing most football activities. He remained manager until 1921 when ill-health brought about his retirement, although he remained with the club as assistant to his successor John Chapman.

John Chapman
1921–26
Honours: None

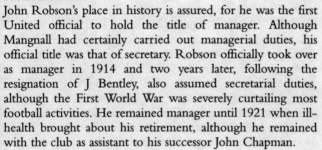

On the basis of football facts alone, John Chapman had a torrid time at United. He arrived at the club from Airdrieonians and could do little to raise the spirit within Old Trafford. Indeed, the club won only one of his first 15 games in charge and ended the season being relegated. Although Chapman got them back into the top flight three years later as runners-up and took them to an FA Cup Semi-Final, that represented the peak of his career. In October 1926, United were informed via a letter from the FA that it was alleged their manager was guilty of improper conduct while carrying out his duties and was to be suspended from all involvement with football with immediate effect. Although full details of the alleged charges were never made public, United had little option but to accede to the FA's directive and dismiss Chapman immediately.

Clarence Hilditch
1926–27
Honours: None

Clarence Hilditch is similarly assured of his place in United's history, for he remains the only player–manager the club have ever appointed. His elevation to such lofty ranks was little more than a stop-gap appointment while United came to terms with having to dismiss Chapman. However, Hilditch took the managerial side of his duties rather too seriously, refusing to select himself as a player when his influence would probably have been more effective on the pitch. When Herbert Bamlett was appointed in 1927, Hilditch resumed his playing career and continued to serve United with distinction until 1932.

Herbert Bamlett
1927–31
Honours: None

When United appointed Herbert Bamlett as manager in 1927 he had an undoubted football pedigree, for he had already managed Oldham Athletic, Wigan Borough and Middlesbrough. However, with all due respect to those clubs, he was not, with hindsight, the right man for the job, for prior to becoming a manager he had made his name as a referee (he was the youngest man to referee a Cup Final, being only 32 when he took charge of Burnley and Liverpool in 1914)! His four seasons at Old Trafford achieved little and at the end of his final campaign United were relegated to the Second Division.

Walter Crickmer
1931–32 and 1937–45
Honours: None

Although he was never officially manager, Walter Crickmer twice assumed the responsibilities, taking charge following the departure of Bamlett and the subsequent arrival of Duncan and taking over again when he resigned in 1937. Two years later League football was suspended by the Second World War, but Crickmer kept the club going during hostilities and ensured as smooth a handover as was possible when Matt Busby arrived in 1945. One of the finest servants the club has ever had, he lost his life in the 1958 Munich air crash.

'Archie' Duncan
1932–37
Honours: Division Two Champions   1935–36

Duncan arrived at United in August 1932 (on a reported salary of £800 per annum) and spent big, bringing in several players from north of the border. Both the media and United's followers expected a more immediate return on their investment than they got, and criticism soon followed when United continued to struggle. He managed to get them into the First Division as Second Division Champions in 1936 and was offered a five-year contract as a result. But United struggled back in the top flight and after 14 games of the 1937–38 season Duncan resigned and moved into the Southern League to become manager of Ipswich Town.

Sir Matt Busby
1945–69 and 1970–71

Honours:	Division One Champions	1951–52, 1955–56, 1956–57, 1964–65, 1966–67
	FA Cup winners	1947–48, 1962–63
	FA Cup runners–up	1956–57, 1957–58
	European Cup winners	1967–68

There is so much Matt Busby achieved with United that it is difficult to know quite where to start; five League Championships (and seven times runners–up), two FA Cup wins (and twice runners–up), the European Cup and countless FA Charity Shields confirm him as one of the greatest managers of all time, but it is the realisation that he began from scratch and went on to build two sides that will forever be remembered as among the greatest to have represented United that is a true epitaph for Busby. For when appointed in 1945 United had no ground, Old Trafford having suffered extensive bomb damage during the Second World War and were forced to share Maine Road.

From such depths Busby lifted United to their current position; the most famous club side in the world. Undoubtedly his crowning glory was the deliverance of the European Cup in 1968, for he had produced a side in the 1950s that might have achieved the honour, only to see them perish at Munich. Patiently and meticulously he set about rebuilding and ten years later realised the dream that had obsessed all United's followers since 1955; winning the European Cup.

Jimmy Murphy
1958
Honours: None

No review of Manchester United's managers would be complete without mention of Jimmy Murphy, Busby's assistant who took over the reigns of the club in the immediate aftermath of the Munich air disaster while Busby himself lay close to death in hospital. Indeed, Murphy only missed being with the United squad because he was on international duty with Wales at the time.

Although Murphy faced a monumental task, unsure of how many players were alive, fit or would ever play again and needing some immediate signings just to ensure United turned out with a full 11, his role in lifting United from the depths of their deepest despair to reaching the FA Cup Final, the European Cup Semi-Final and a credible League position should not be overlooked.

Wilf McGuinness
1969–70
Honours: None

When Matt Busby made his decision to retire from the cut and thrust of everyday League management, the unenviable task of replacing a legend fell to club coach Wilf McGuinness. Although McGuinness had served United for almost 17 years in various capacities, little prepared him for the daunting task of managing a club where expectations always run high. History will show that despite some minor success (three Semi-Finals in the two domestic Cup competitions), replacing Busby was one task that was beyond him.

Frank O'Farrell
1971–72
Honours: None

Having tried unsuccessfully to find a successor for Matt Busby within Old Trafford, the club looked externally and took O'Farrell from Leicester, where his achievements on a shoestring budget and reputation as a 'nice man' had not gone unnoticed. Ultimately, his niceness probably worked against him, for a firmer hand might have prevented George Best from going absent without leave on numerous occasions. O'Farrell could do little about the likes of Bobby Charlton reaching the end of their careers, but the replacements were pale shadows of the greats who had represented United in the past. Both O'Farrell and his assistant Malcolm Musgrove were sacked in December 1972.

Tommy Docherty
1972–77
Honours: Division Two Champions 1974–75
    FA Cup winners   1976–77
    FA Cup runners–up 1975–76

The arrival of the charismatic Tommy Docherty at Old Trafford would eventually provide a breath of fresh air to United, but not before relegation to the Second Division had been suffered. In truth, the slide did United little harm, for crowds remained constant and, more importantly, regular wins in the lower division did wonders for morale. Upon return to the higher flight, it was business as usual and United were back in contention for the title. As it was, Docherty was only able to deliver one trophy, the FA Cup (victory achieved one year after finishing runners–up to Southampton in the same competition), but his subsequent dismissal concerned his off-field activities rather than his team's performance on it, for the revelation that he was having an affair with the wife of one of the backroom staff hastened his departure.

Dave Sexton
1977–81
Honours: FA Cup runners-up   1978–79

Following Docherty's unceremonious departure the need for a steady, reliable man to take the helm at one of the top clubs in the country was paramount, and Dave Sexton's appointment was widely viewed as an attempt to present a more acceptable face in the wake of the scandal that had surrounded Docherty's dismissal. Sexton arrived with excellent credentials; as coach with Chelsea and QPR he had turned both clubs into effective forces within the game, although it was only with Chelsea that he had managed to pick up the game's higher honours.

Sadly, he was unable to repeat that success at United, despite spending vast amounts of money on a number of players who would later have an important part to play in United's success. It was felt he was too distant from his players, although there was no doubting his coaching abilities.

Ron Atkinson
1981–86

Honours: FA Cup winners   1982–83, 1984–85
           League Cup runners–up   1982–83

In many ways the appointment of Ron Atkinson mirrored that of Tommy Docherty; a larger-than-life character who would impose his own personality and authority upon the club. As Atkinson was unable to deliver the one trophy that United and their followers treasured above all others, the League Championship, his spell might be viewed as a failure, but two FA Cup wins and almost constant battle for higher honours tells a different story.

At almost any other club such success would be viewed differently, but having spent considerable sums of money on individual players, including a record breaking £1.5 million on Bryan Robson and £1.1 million on Frank Stapleton, his inability to deliver the League title ultimately counted against him. After a record breaking opening to the 1985–86 season and building up a seemingly unassailable lead, a final finish of fourth place was deemed unacceptable and Atkinson was dismissed.

Alex Ferguson
1986–(97)

Honours: Premier League Champions   1992-93, 1993-94, 1995-96, 1996-97

     FA Cup winners   1989-90, 1993-94, 1995-96

     FA Cup runners–up   1994-95

     League Cup winners   1991-92

     League Cup runners–up   1990-91, 1993-94

     European Cup Winners' Cup winners   1990-91

The arrival of Aberdeen manager Alex Ferguson into the Old Trafford hot seat was viewed with hesitation by some; although he had done extremely well in breaking the Glasgow domination in Scotland, south of the border he was an unknown quantity. And, after his first four years had promised much but delivered little in terms of silverware, there were many who felt he had had his time and failed.

Since then everything Ferguson has touched has turned to silver; four League titles, three FA Cups, a League Cup and the European Cup Winners' Cup have all arrived in the Old Trafford trophy room (including the coveted Double of FA Cup and League Championship on two occasions), leaving only the European Cup as the ultimate prize required. And, as if such cup collecting was not enough, Ferguson has completely transformed United, rebuilding the youth set-up so that they now produce a high percentage of their own players.

In terms of honours won he has already surpassed Matt Busby, but it is now the European Cup that United treasure more than anything else. Victory in this tournament will surely elevate Alex Ferguson into the ranks of the greatest.

BEST SEASON 2

The 1967–68 campaign ranks as perhaps the best season in United's history because it ended in triumph in the one competition which had transfixed both its manager and its followers above all others; the European Cup.

That said, there were times when United looked likely to make it a unique Double of the European Cup and retention of their League title; perhaps the vision of success at Wembley in the major competition caused concentration to dip below the usual high standards.

United began the season with a defeat against Everton but quickly settled into their stride, steadily moving up the table and making headway on the early pace-setters, including great rivals Manchester City. United drew first blood against their rivals too, winning the clash at Maine Road in September 2-1. By the time the New Year celebrations had died down the title race had effectively become a three-horse race between City, United and Liverpool, with Leeds United poised should any of their Lancashire rivals falter.

United showed little sign of faltering until March, when the twin assault on domestic and European success began to take its toll. Having suffered only three defeats in their opening 28 games (Everton on the opening day, Forest and and Leeds), warnings of the Ides of March began to ring true. Burnley inflicted a narrow defeat in February, and then successive defeats against Chelsea and Coventry, followed by revenge for Manchester City before the month was out, began to derail the United train.

Although Liverpool came to Old Trafford for the opening fixture in April and returned home with both points, a further four unbeaten games put United back in the driving seat. Unfortunately, two defeats in their final three games gave City the title by two points; a victory in either game would have been enough to keep the trophy at Old Trafford.

By April however attention had switched from the domestic battle to success on the European front. Victories over Hibernian of Malta, FK Sarajevo, Gornik Zabrze and Real Madrid ensured United's presence at Wembley. The events of that evening are covered elsewhere in this book, but lifting the European Cup after a journey that had began over ten years previously was the crowning glory on this, the most perfect of seasons.

1967-68 LEAGUE RECORD

Opponents	Home	Away
Arsenal	1-0	2-0
Burnley	2-2	1-2
Chelsea	1-3	1-1
Coventry City	4-0	0-2
Everton	3-1	1-3
Fulham	3-0	4-0
Leeds United	1-0	0-1
Leicester City	1-1	2-2
Liverpool	1-2	2-1
Manchester City	1-3	2-1
Newcastle United	6-0	2-2
Nottingham Forest	3-0	1-3
Sheffield United	1-0	3-0
Sheffield Wednesday	4-2	1-1
Southampton	3-2	2-2
Stoke City	1-0	4-2
Sunderland	1-2	1-1
Tottenham Hotspur	3-1	2-1
West Bromwich Albion	2-1	3-6
West Ham United	3-1	3-1
Wolverhampton Wanderers	4-0	3-2

THE GROUNDS

Manchester United have had three official homes, as well as one unofficial home, during their history. When the club was formed as Newton Heath in 1878 they played on the edge of a clay-pit at North Road, Monsall, with the changing rooms located half a mile away at the Three Crowns public house.

While the Heathens played little more than friendlies against local opposition such premises were deemed acceptable, although when the club was admitted to the Football League in 1892 both the state of the pitch and the need for decent changing facilities necessitated a proper ground. The club duly moved to Clayton, taking up residence at Bank Street. In truth, the pitch was little better than the one they had left behind and the massive chimneys that surrounded the area provided a surreal backdrop.

Thanks to the club's first major benefactor, a Mr Davies, investing £500, a 1,000-seater stand was built and the club's fortunes seemed to be on the upturn, for in 1904 the ground was chosen to host the Football League match against their Scottish counterparts. Even so, the club had greater designs and, with Davies donating the then-massive sum of £60,000, the search began for a new plot that could be developed into the finest ground in the country. In 1909 United sold their home at Clayton to the Manchester Corporation for £5,000, although plans for their new home at the site of Trafford Park were not due to be discussed until the following week! Stretford Council duly approved the plans for an 80,000 capacity ground to be called Old Trafford.

The plans submitted and approved were grand to say the least. In addition to an 80,000 capacity, the luxuries that were to be installed offered the very best; tea-rooms, tip-up seats and attendants to show spectators to them, a fully equipped gymnasium, games rooms and a plunge bath for the players. United bade farewell to their Clayton home in January 1910 with a 5-0 win over Spurs, a month later playing host to Liverpool at Old Trafford for the first time and narrowly losing a seven-goal thriller.

Although Old Trafford could boast an 80,000 capacity (and how they could do with that kind of figure now!) it was never filled, the highest attendance being the 76,962 who witnessed an FA Cup Semi-Final in 1939. Following extensive bomb damage during a German raid, United found a temporary home with City at Maine Road. At the end of the war United were awarded £22,278 by the War Damage Commission and plans were announced that would bring the capacity up to 120,000, but the club lacked the required funds and therefore only redeveloped the Main Stand. The club returned to their spiritual home in 1949 for their first Football League match in ten years.

Since then Old Trafford has been transformed into the finest club ground in the country. A massive cantilever stand was added in 1964 in preparation for the forthcoming World Cup in 1966, and since then the roof has been continued around the ground, in stages, to provide cover for all patrons. United's run of success during the 1990s and the thousands of disappointed fans who could not gain access prompted the building of an additional tier opposite the Main Stand, bringing the capacity up to 56,000. Even this was not sufficient to accommodate all those wishing to pay homage, so don't discount similar tiers being added around the ground.

THROUGH THE YEARS
JULY

1977
July
4

United sacked manager Tommy Docherty for 'breach of contract' after it was revealed he was having an affair with the wife of physiotherapist Laurie Brown. Docherty had been a charismatic manager at Old Trafford, winning the FA Cup and taking United to the Second Division Championship during his tenure, although the revelation of his affair left the club with little option but to sack him. Docherty's comment at the time was 'I have been punished for falling in love. What I have done has got nothing at all to do with my track record as a manager.'

1989
July
15

Laurie Cunningham, the second black player to be capped by England, was killed in a car crash near Madrid after returning from a nightclub. The former Leyton Orient, West Bromwich Albion and Manchester United star picked up an FA Cup winner's medal as substitute for Wimbledon in 1988 and won six England caps, the last of which came while he was playing for Real Madrid.

1966
July
30

Bobby Charlton and Nobby Stiles play their part in England's finest hour – a 4-2 World Cup Final win against West Germany at Wembley. Little did anyone know at that point that United would be returning to that venue two years later to claim the ultimate European club prize.

1993
July
22

Fiery 21-year-old Irishman Roy Keane signs for United from Nottingham Forest, the fee £3.75 million. He would go on to make the midfield motorman's position at Old Trafford his own in succession to Bryan Robson, adding many more international caps to his tally, before a late-1997 injury kept him out for almost an entire season.

ATTENDANCES

As befits the most popular (and successful!) club in the country, United's Old Trafford home is currently the largest club ground in the country. Its history, and that of the crowds who have flocked to see the team are equally impressive.

The largest crowd ever gathered inside Old Trafford was not, however, to see United but an FA Cup Semi-Final between Wolverhampton Wanderers and Grimsby Town in March 1939, with 76,962 seeing Wolves move on to Wembley. The largest crowd to have watched Manchester United at Old Trafford had been recorded in 1920 when Aston Villa were the visitors, with 70,504 attending the Christmas fixture which the visitors won 3-1.

Interestingly, it was not until 1925 that clubs had to inform the Football League of their actual gate figures (such information was then required because both the League and the visiting clubs were entitled to a percentage based on the crowd figure) and many crowd figures published previously are usually estimates made by newspaper reporters in attendance. The local newspaper that covered this particular match, for example, published an estimated crowd figure of 45,000, over 25,000 fewer than were actually present!

Of course, even this is not the largest crowd to have witnessed a Manchester United home League match, for in 1948, while United were playing at City's Maine Road ground, their own home being rebuilt following bomb damage, a crowd of 83,260 attended the game between United and Arsenal on 17 January 1948. The match finished all-square at 1-1.

It has also often been quoted that Old Trafford witnessed the lowest ever League crowd when only 13 people paid to watch Stockport versus Leicester City in a Division Two game on 7 May 1921 – but this has since been discredited, as contemporary newspaper reports put the figure at approximately 2,000.

Not unsurprisingly, Manchester United also hold the record for the highest aggregate crowd figure in a season and the highest average; a total of 1,212,900 watched their home League campaign in 1967-68, an average of 57,758. This beat the previous record held by Newcastle, whose average of 56,351 in 1947-48 had been achieved in the Second Division. The attraction of United also holds good away from home, for seven current League clubs have recorded their highest attendances when United have been the visitors.

Aside from the aforementioned Wolves-Grimsby FA Cup clash, Old Trafford has also hosted FA Cup Final replays (the last being in 1970 between Chelsea and Leeds which drew 62,000 spectators), League Cup Final replays (Aston Villa and Everton attracting 54,749 in 1977) and various international matches. During the 1996 European Championships, Old Trafford was second only to Wembley as the chief venue of the competition, hosting group, Quarter-Final and Semi-Final matches. The highest attendance recorded at Old Trafford during the competition was the 50,760 that saw Germany beat Romania 3-0.

DREAM TEAM 2

United's 1968 triumph in becoming the first English club to win the European Cup has inspired every League Champion since and ensured every one of those who took part in the Wembley Final booked their place in United's roll of honour.

STEPNEY **1**

BRENNAN **2** CRERAND **4** FOULKES **5** DUNNE **3**

BEST **7** STILES **6** SADLER **10** ASTON **11**

KIDD **8** CHARLTON **9**

Goalkeeper   **Alex Stepney**

Began his professional career with Millwall in 1963 and made nearly 150 appearances before a £50,000 switch to Stamford Bridge. He made only one appearance for Chelsea before signing for United for £55,000 and immediately established himself as first choice, winning a League medal and European Cup medals in successive seasons. Finished his United career in 1978.

Right-back   **Shay Brennan**

One of youngsters pressed into service following the decimation of the side at Munich, Irishman Brennan went on to give sterling service to United and made over 300 appearances for the club. Won two League Championship medals and a European Cup winner's medal.

Left-back   **Tony Dunne**

Established himself as a United regular during the 1961-62 season and made over 500 appearances for the club before signing with Bolton in 1973 and taking his senior appearances tally to 600 matches. He moved to America in 1979.

Right-half   **Pat Crerand**

Began his professional career with Celtic and was signed by United for £56,000 in February 1963, finishing the season with an FA Cup winner's medal. Collected two League titles and a European Cup medal and joined United's ground staff when he retired from playing in 1971.

Centre-half   **Bill Foulkes**

He joined United as an amateur in 1949 and was elevated to the professional ranks, making his United debut in 1952. A regular from the following season, he was a survivor of the Munich crash and by the time he packed up playing in the 1969–70 season, had made over 600 first-team appearances. Won four League titles and an FA Cup winner's medal in addition to his European medal.

Left-half   **Nobby Stiles**

Along with team-mate Bobby Charlton, Nobby Stiles won three of the game's greatest honours in three seasons: a World Cup winner's medal, League Championship and European Cup medal. A tough tackling no-nonsense player, he made over 300 United appearances.

Outside-right   **George Best**

Perhaps one of the finest footballing talents since the Second World War, George Best achieved much in a short space of time. But for the retirement of Sir Matt Busby and Best's decline thereafter, he might have gone on to become even more of a legend. As it was, he made over 400 appearances in a United shirt, was Footballer of the Year and European Player of the Year at the height of his career but subsequently retired in 1974. Later appeared for Fulham and several other clubs.

Inside-right   **Brian Kidd**

The aptly-named Brian Kidd celebrated his 19th birthday in the best possible style; scoring in United's European Cup

Final victory. Moved on to Arsenal for £110,000 in 1974 and later appeared for Manchester City, Everton and Bolton. Is currently assistant to Alex Ferguson.

Centre-forward   Bobby Charlton

One of the greatest names in world football, Bobby Charlton's career took in everything that was good in the game – the highest honours and accolades, a success for both club and country and all conducted in a sportsmanlike fashion. He made his United debut in 1956 and by the time he retired in 1973 had helped himself to just about every honour imaginable; three League titles, an FA Cup winner's medal, a European Cup medal and, with England, a World Cup winner's medal.

Inside-left   David Sadler

Joined United in the face of fierce competition for his signature in 1962 and made his debut the following year. He could play equally well at centre-forward and centre-half, but was probably happier in a defensive role. Moved on to Preston in 1973 and remained at Deepdale until 1977 when injury forced his retirement.

Outside-left   John Aston

The son of John Aston Snr, who played for United between 1946 and 1954, John Aston Jnr made his debut in 1965 and went on to make over 150 appearances until a broken leg ended his Old Trafford career. He resumed with Luton, Mansfield and Blackburn before retiring in the late 1970s.

MUFC TRIVIA QUIZ

How much do you know about the Red Devils? Answers on page 190–191.

1 In 1968 United became the first English side to win the European Cup, but who did they beat in the Semi-Final over two legs?

2 Against which side did Bobby Charlton score his first League goals for United?

3 Who were United's first opponents following the Munich air disaster?

4 Against whom did Peter Schmeichel score for United in the UEFA Cup?

5 In which season did United first win the FA Cup?

6 And in which season did they first win the League Championship?

7 What is the record Old Trafford attendance?

8 What is the record attendance at Old Trafford for a match involving Manchester United?

9 Kevin Moran became the first player sent off in an FA Cup Final, but on whom did he attempt the tackle that led to his dismissal?

10   United's only League Cup Final victory came in 1992 when the competition was known as the Rumbelows Cup. Who did they beat?

11   Although United entered the very first League Cup competition, they then declined entry for a number of years. In which season did they make their second appearance?

12   Mark Hughes has won four FA Cup winner's medals, but how many did he collect with United?

13   Manchester United were the first club side to have topped the national pop charts, but with which record?

14   When was the last season United won the old Second Division title?

15   United won the European Super Cup in 1991, but who did they beat?

16   Which were the only two clubs to win at Old Trafford in the League during the 1996–97 season?

17   And which were the only three sides to inflict defeat on United away from home that season?

18   As well as having won the FA Cup on more occasions than any other club, United also hold the record for the most number of appearances in the final. How many exactly?

19   Alex Ferguson is one of only two managers to have led clubs on both sides of the border to the FA Cup. How many Scottish FA Cups did he win with Aberdeen?

20   Eight of United's FA Cup Final victories have come at Wembley. Where was the other match played?

21   How many appearances in FA Cup Semi-Finals have Manchester United made?

22   Who was the last United player to be named the Football Writers' Association Player of the Year?

23   Who was the last United player to be named PFA Player of the Year?

24   Ryan Giggs is the only player to have retained his award as PFA Young Player of the Year. In which two years did he achieve this feat?

25   Who was the last United player to be named European Footballer of the Year?

26   Who was the last United player to make his competitive debut in a match against Manchester City?

27   How many League titles have United won (the old First Division and the Premiership combined)?

28   United's biggest Premiership win of 1996–97 was 5–0. Who was this against?

29   To whom did they lose 5–0 the same season?

30 Peter Schmeichel missed only two Premiership games during season 1996-97; who replaced him?

31 Who were United's last opponents at their ground at Bank Street, Clayton?

32 When United beat Ipswich Town 9-0 in 1995 and Andy Cole scored five goals, only one other player scored more than one goal. Who?

33 Combining the Premiership and the old First Division, how many times have United finished runners-up?

34 Who scored United's four goals when they won the European Cup in 1968?

35 Who did United play in their first European Cup tie?

36 How many European Cup Semi-Finals have United played?

37 What was the result of the most recent City v United derby match, played on 6 April 1996?

38 Where were United playing when they won the title in season 1995-96?

39 What is the highest number of League goals United have scored in a season?

40 Who is United's record League scorer in a season and how many did he score?

THROUGH THE YEARS
AUGUST

1970
August
5

United and Hull City became the first clubs to take part in a penalty shoot-out when their Watney Cup Semi-Final ended all square at 1-1. United won the shoot out 4-3 to advance but were beaten by Derby County. United later became the first Premiership side to be beaten in the FA Cup by a penalty shoot-out when they lost to Southampton.

1974
August
5

Maverick United star George Best made his debut appearance for non-League Dunstable Town in a friendly against United's reserves, helping Dunstable to a 3-2 win.

1967
August
12

United as League Champions played host to FA Cup winners Spurs in the Charity Shield at Old Trafford, one of Spurs' goals in a 3-3 draw coming from keeper Pat Jennings! A massive clearance aimed at Alan Gilzean caught Alex Stepney unawares and the ball bounced over him into the net. In 1975 Alex was in the news again when he suffered the strangest injury ever sustained on a football field – he dislocated his jaw while shouting at his team mates!

1912
August
18

Ernest Mangnall, United's most sucessful manager until the advent of Matt Busby, shocked Manchester and the football world by quitting Old Trafford for rivals City.

1989
August
14

Ray Wilkins was reunited with former Chelsea manager – now United boss – Dave Sexton in a £850,000 deal. It was good business, since the England midfielder gave five years' service before being sold to AC Milan for £1.5 million.

TRANSFERS

As befits the biggest club in the game, United have never been afraid to spend big on the right players, breaking the transfer record in 1981 in order to land Bryan Robson from West Brom for £1.5 million.

While Robson's transfer was not unexpected, little prepared United's followers for the bombshell that greeted them when they awoke on 10 January 1995. Andy Cole had been a key figure in the resurgence of Newcastle United, scoring goals almost at will and slotting easily into a system that suited his style of play perfectly. And yet, for some reason, Kevin Keegan was prepared to let him go, agreeing a fee of £7 million with Alex Ferguson, made up of £6 million and winger Keith Gillespie.

If the news caused both glee and astonishment at Old Trafford, there was nearly a riot at St James Park! This transfer, at the time the record transfer deal between two English clubs, stunned the football world and in an instant took an already awesome front line into another dimension.

It has to be said that Cole took time to settle into the United side; some even said he was something of a misfit. But while Newcastle had specifically played to his strengths, at Old Trafford he had to fit into a team pattern. But he has developed into more of an all-round team player, scoring and creating goals. Much of the credit for this should go to Teddy Sheringham, whose £3 million switch from Spurs was another of Alex's swoops on the transfer market and whose speed of mind more than compensates for any lack of pace.

As much as Alex Ferguson is a buying manager, eager to bring in any player who he feels will improve his side, he is not afraid to dismantle at the same time, selling players who could possibly still give United good service – would any other manager have sold Mark Hughes, Paul Ince or Steve Bruce? More than anything, there was reason behind each of these decisions, and while Mark and Paul have showed little sign of losing their effectiveness within the game, the replacements brought in have proved more than capable.

While Cole remains United's most expensive purchase, the £7 million United received from Internazionale of Milan represents the most expensive sale. There were many who felt Ince would return to Old Trafford when after two years he looked to return home to England, but Ferguson chose not to invoke the clause in Paul's contract that gave United first option on his transfer. As United surged back to the top of the table before Christmas, he was proved once again to have made the right decision.

There is one transfer Alex Ferguson would have dearly loved to have pulled off, one which would have lifted the record transfer fee to some £15 million, and that was Alan Shearer. When it became clear Shearer would be leaving Blackburn Rovers he was one of the first managers to be given permission to talk to the player and offer terms. By all accounts, Alan Shearer was convinced he was just one signature away from becoming a United player, but at the 11th hour Newcastle got their man.

Rumour has it the final decision was taken by Blackburn benefactor Jack Walker, who felt it would not be in Blackburn's interests selling to their chief rivals for the Championship – but, since the arrival of Shearer at Newcastle has turned them into potential Champions, the argument doesn't really hold up. As it is, United will have to get along with a striking force of Cole, Sheringham, Scholes, Solskjaer *et al*!

WORST SEASON 2

Those who had prayed for a speedy return to the top flight following the ignominy of relegation in 1931 were to be sadly disappointed, for United found it hard to find their footing in the Second Division.

If the mood over Old Trafford had been gloomy following relegation, then it went from bad to worse, for United also found themselves facing severe financial pressure. The bank refused to extend the overdraft and there was a real worry the players would not be paid. The arrival of local businessman James Gibson seemed to have saved the day, for over the next two seasons money was made available for new players, new manager 'Archie' Scott Duncan spending over £20,000 to bring in fresh blood to take United to promotion.

As it happened Duncan very nearly did take United out of the Second Division – straight into the Third! Once again, a poor start at the beginning of the season let them down and left them with a mountain to climb, with the first victory not arriving until the sixth game and only two of the opening five games yielding any points at all. Two straight wins lifted the gloom for a time, but inconsistency all season was to almost cost United dearly.

As the season progressed the shape of the division became apparent; Grimsby, Preston, Bolton and Brentford would be contesting the promotion spots, whilst United would be down at the other end, fighting with the likes of Lincoln, Millwall, Swansea, Notts County and Nottingham Forest against relegation.

By the time the clubs entered the home straight in April, the situation for United looked perilous, for although they finished March with a rare win, 2-0 at home to Blackpool, and Lincoln were effectively relegated, any one of the other five sides could still go down with them. Defeat at West Ham was followed by a draw at Bradford City. Then United got a vital win, 2-0 at home to Port Vale, leaving three fixtures which would decide their fate – Notts County away, Swansea at home and Millwall away on the last day of the season.

When both County and Swansea managed to force draws and save themselves in the process, it left United having to win at Millwall in order to retain their Second Division status. A 2-0 win was achieved but a final position of 20th in the Second Division remains the club's lowest ever.

1933-34 LEAGUE RECORD

Opponents	Home	Away
Blackpool	2-0	1-3
Bolton Wanderers	1-5	1-3
Bradford	0-4	1-6
Bradford City	2-1	1-1
Brentford	1-3	4-3
Burnley	5-2	4-1
Bury	2-1	1-2
Fulham	1-0	2-0
Grimsby Town	1-3	3-7
Hull City	4-1	1-4
Lincoln City	1-1	1-5
Millwall	1-1	2-0
Nottingham Forest	0-1	1-1
Notts County	1-2	0-0
Oldham	2-3	0-2
Plymouth Argyle	0-3	0-4
Port Vale	2-0	3-2
Preston North End	1-0	2-3
Southampton	1-0	0-1
Swansea	1-1	1-2
West Ham United	0-1	1-2

A-Z OF UNITED

From aggregate and Anderlecht to the zenith of European glory – it's all here!

A United's record aggregate score in European competition is the 12-0 victory over Anderlecht, a score achieved in United's very first European campaign. They won 2-0 away and 10-0 at home.

B United's best start to a season in recent times was in season 1985-86 with 13 victories and two draws in their opening 15 games.

C The current capacity of Old Trafford is 56,387, the largest club capacity in England.

D United's record defeat is 0-7, which was achieved by Blackburn Rovers in 1926, Aston Villa in 1930 and Wolves in 1931.

E United have won two European trophies during their history; the 1968 European Cup and the 1991 European Cup Winners' Cup.

F In the history of the FA Cup no club has been more successful than United. Their victory over Liverpool in 1996 was their ninth win in the competition, one more than Spurs.

G The most goals scored by United in a season is 103, achieved in 1956-57 and 1958-59.

H The first home match at Old Trafford was against Liverpool on 19 February 1910 and saw United lose 3-4. H is also for hat-tricks, with Robert Donaldson scoring the club's first League hat-trick in the 1892-93 while the club were still known as Newton Heath.

I Bobby Charlton has won more international caps than any other United player, having been picked for England on 106 occasions.

J John Davies was an early benefactor of Newton Heath. Legend has it he came across a St Bernard dog belonging to club captain Harry Stafford which had been sent around a bazaar with a collecting box around its neck, so desperate were the club for funds. Davies injected £3,000 in order to keep them afloat.

K United have kits for every occasion – and while the number they have introduced in quick succession in recent years has attracted adverse publicity, they still sell more replica strips than any other club.

L United's biggest League victory was achieved on 15 October 1892 when Newton Heath beat Wolves 10-1. Their biggest as United was achieved in 1995 when they beat Ipswich Town 9-0.

M United's record League marksman in aggregate is Bobby Charlton who scored 199 goals between 1956 and 1973. Dennis Viollet scored 32 in season 1959-60 to hold the record for a single season.

N United's traditional nickname is the Red Devils, as indicated on the club's badge.

O In 1923 Sam Wynne, playing for Oldham, scored two own goals and two goals for Oldham in their 3-2 win over Manchester United!

P The highest number of points under the old two points for a win system was 64 achieved in 1956-57. Under three points for a win, United's highest total was 92 in 1993-94.

Q In the 1896-97 FA Cup competition, Newton Heath had to play four Qualifying Round matches before taking their place in the First Round. They finally reached the Third Round proper before losing 0-2 to Derby.

R The club record receipts are £739,841 for the European Cup Champions League match held on 23 April 1997.

S The Screen Sport Super Cup was a competition for clubs who would have qualified for European competition in 1985-86 had there not been a post-Heysel ban. United made four appearances in the tournament, drawing two and losing two matches.

T The highest transfer fee paid is the £7 million total (£6 million in cash and Keith Gillespie, valued at £1 million) it cost to bring Andy Cole to Old Trafford, and the highest transfer fee received is also £7 million, for Paul Ince from Inter Milan.

U United's best performance in the UEFA Cup was in season 1984-85 when they reached the Fourth Round, losing to Videoton 5-4 on penalties after the tie had finished 1-1 on aggregate.

V United's highest number of victories in the FA Premier League came in 1993-94, when they won 27 of their 42 League games (Blackburn equalled the record the following season).

W United won 14 consecutive League matches in season 1904-05, the joint best winning sequence in the old Second Division.

X Xmas Day matches are unknown today. The last time United were called upon to play one was in 1957 when they beat Luton Town 3-0 at Old Trafford. The following day the two sides drew 2-2 at Kenilworth Road.

Y United have one of the most successful records in the FA Youth Cup, winning the trophy the first five times following its inauguration.

Z The zenith of United's history was the European Cup win of 1968, the culmination of a ten-year dream.

THROUGH THE YEARS
SEPTEMBER

1946
September
30

Johnny Carey was capped by Northern Ireland in their match against England at Belfast. After the game he travelled down to Dublin where two days later he was picked by Eire, again against England! This is one of most celebrated examples of a player having dual nationality. Eight months later Carey was also selected by the Rest of Europe for their match against Great Britain.

1956
September
12

United made their debut appearance in European competition with a 2-1 win against Anderlecht in Brussels, Dennis Viollet and Tommy Taylor grabbing the goals. The return leg in Manchester saw United score ten goals without reply, establishing a British record score for the competition.

1963
September
14

George Best made his debut for United in the 1-0 win at home against West Bromwich Albion, David Sadler scoring the only goal in front of 50,453 spectators.

1977
September
14

United were thrown out of the European Cup Winners' Cup following crowd violence at the match at St Etienne, although they were subsequently reinstated and ordered to play the return leg at Plymouth.

1990
September
4

Steve Bruce became the first First Division player to be dismissed for a so-called 'professional foul' when he was sent off during United's 1-0 win at Luton.

BOGEY TEAMS

For the last 50 or 60 years, Manchester United have been the plum draw for any side in Cup competitions. The dream of playing at Old Trafford in front of a full house, irrespective of whether 90 per cent of those present are rooting for the home side, is still one that makes the FA Cup such a magical event.

During 1952–53, Walthamstow Avenue's reward for battling their way past Wimbledon, Watford and Stockport was the lip-smacking prospect of a visit to Old Trafford to play the League Champions. Although their Cup run was sure to come to an end, they would at least pick up a bumper payday. But things didn't go quite the way the script demanded, for they raised their game for the encounter.

Walthamstow emerged after 90 minutes with an astonishing draw, earning an even more lucrative replay after the sides had finished all square with one goal apiece. Such was the demand to see the replay Walthamstow wisely took the decision to switch the game to Highbury, where 49,119 finally saw United's class win out with a 5-2 victory. United's luck ran out in the following round, Everton winning 2-1.

That Walthamstow episode is perhaps the closest United have come since the Second World War to suffering a major Cup upset, although there have been one or two embarrassing results over the years, with Walsall's victory in 1975 perhaps the pick of the bunch. The Saddlers had battled to earn a replay after the first meeting at Old Trafford and finally finished off the job after extra time, winning 3-2.

With nine trophy wins so far, United are the most successful club in the FA Cup's history. The closest scare they had, however, came in the 1983 Final against underdogs Brighton & Hove Albion, less than two months after United had narrowly lost to Liverpool in the League Cup Final. Brighton were already relegated from the First Division by the time they strode out at Wembley (having arrived at the ground via helicopter – the team were determined to enjoy their day, regardless of the outcome) but found form which had been beyond them during the League campaign.

At 2-2 and with extra time drawing to a close, Gordon Smith was presented with a golden opportunity to settle the game in Brighton's favour and only a miraculous save from Gary Bailey kept United in the hunt. They made no mistakes five nights later, netting four goals with no reply to take the trophy with the biggest winning margin since Bury beat Derby 6-0 80 years earlier.

It's only since the 1990s that United have begun to get to grips with the Football League Cup, winning once and finishing runners-up twice, along with the aforementioned defeat in 1983. The club's early efforts were not of the same calibre, with a 5-1 mauling at Blackpool in 1966-67 (the year United finished League Champions!), a Semi-Final defeat by then Third Division Aston Villa in 1970-71 and a home defeat by Bristol Rovers in 1972-73 (despite the likes of Charlton, Best and Kidd in the United line-up) among the horror stories most fans try to forget. More recently, a 3-0 home defeat against York was sustained while on the way to a 4-3 aggregate defeat in 1995-96.

Such major upsets are the exception rather than the rule, although Alex Ferguson's habit of not treating the League Cup too seriously when there is the European Cup to worry about, does mean that more upsets could be on the cards.

LEAGUE RECORD

After a barren spell during the 1970s and 1980s, United claimed the Premiership title four times in its first five seasons.

Season	Division	P	W	D	L	F-A	Pts	Pos
1892-93	One	30	6	6	18	50-85	18	16th
1893-94	One	30	6	2	22	36-72	14	16th
Relegated								
1894-95	Two	30	15	8	7	78-44	38	3rd
1895-96	Two	30	15	3	12	66-57	33	6th
1896-97	Two	30	17	5	8	56-34	39	2nd
Division Two Runners-up								
1897-98	Two	30	16	6	8	64-35	38	4th
1898-99	Two	34	19	5	10	67-43	43	4th
1899-1900	Two	34	20	4	10	63-27	44	4th
1900-01	Two	34	14	4	16	42-38	32	10th
1901-02	Two	34	11	6	17	38-53	28	15th
1902-03	Two	34	15	8	11	53-38	38	5th
1903-04	Two	34	20	8	6	65-33	48	3rd
1904-05	Two	34	24	5	5	81-30	53	3rd
1905-06	Two	38	28	6	4	90-28	62	2nd
Division Two Runners-up								
1906-07	One	38	17	8	13	53-56	42	8th
1907-08	One	38	23	6	9	81-48	52	1st
★ Division One Champions ★								

Season	Division	P	W	D	L	F-A	Pts	Pos
1908-09	One	38	15	7	16	58-68	37	13th
1909-10	One	38	19	7	12	69-61	45	5th
1910-11	One	38	22	8	8	72-40	52	1st
⭐ Division One Champions ⭐								
1911-12	One	38	13	11	14	45-60	37	13th
1912-13	One	38	19	8	11	69-43	46	4th
1913-14	One	38	15	6	17	52-62	36	14th
1914-15	One	38	9	12	17	46-62	30	18th
1919-20	One	42	13	14	15	54-50	40	12th
1920-21	One	42	15	10	17	64-68	40	13th
1921-22	One	42	8	12	22	41-73	28	22nd
Relegated								
1922-23	Two	42	17	14	11	51-36	48	4th
1923-24	Two	42	13	14	15	52-44	40	14th
1924-25	Two	42	23	11	8	57-23	57	2nd
● Division Two Runners-up ●								
1925-26	One	42	19	6	17	66-73	44	9th
1926-27	One	42	13	14	15	52-64	40	15th
1927-28	One	42	16	7	19	72-80	39	18th
1928-29	One	42	14	13	15	66-76	41	12th
1929-30	One	42	15	8	19	67-88	38	17th
1930-31	One	42	7	8	27	53-115	22	22nd
Relegated								
1931-32	Two	42	17	8	17	71-72	42	12th
1932-33	Two	42	15	13	14	71-68	43	6th
1933-34	Two	42	14	6	22	59-85	34	20th
1934-35	Two	42	23	4	15	76-55	50	5th
1935-36	Two	42	22	12	8	85-43	56	1st
⭐ Division Two Champions ⭐								

Season	Division	P	W	D	L	F-A	Pts	Pos
1936–37	One	42	10	12	20	55-78	32	21st
⬤			**Relegated**				⬤	
1937–38	Two	42	22	9	11	82-50	53	2nd
⬤			**Division Two Runners-up**				⬤	
1938–39	One	42	11	16	15	57-65	38	14th
1946–47	One	42	22	12	8	95-54	56	2nd
⬤			**Division One Runners-up**				⬤	
1947–48	One	42	19	14	9	81-48	52	2nd
⬤			**Division One Runners-up**				⬤	
1948–49	One	42	21	11	10	77-44	53	2nd
⬤			**Division One Runners-up**				⬤	
1949–50	One	42	18	14	10	69-44	50	4th
1950–51	One	42	24	8	10	74-40	56	2nd
⬤			**Division One Runners-up**				⬤	
1951–52	One	42	23	11	8	95-52	57	1st
★			**Division One Champions**				★	
1952–53	One	42	18	10	14	69-72	46	8th
1953–54	One	42	18	12	12	73-58	48	4th
1954–55	One	42	20	7	15	84-74	47	5th
1955–56	One	42	25	10	7	83-51	60	1st
★			**Division One Champions**				★	
1956–57	One	42	28	8	6	103-54	64	1st
★			**Division One Champions**				★	
1957–58	One	42	16	11	15	85-75	43	9th

Season	Division	P	W	D	L	F-A	Pts	Pos
1958-59	One	42	24	7	11	103-66	55	2nd
●		Division One Runners-up					●	
1959-60	One	42	19	7	16	102-80	45	7th
1960-61	One	42	18	9	15	88-76	45	7th
1961-62	One	42	15	9	18	72-75	39	15th
1962-63	One	42	12	10	20	67-81	34	19th
1963-64	One	42	23	7	12	90-62	53	2nd
●		Division One Runners-up					●	
1964-65	One	42	26	9	7	89-39	61	1st
★		Division One Champions					★	
1965-66	One	42	18	15	9	84-59	51	4th
1966-67	One	42	24	12	6	84-45	60	1st
★		Division One Champions					★	
1967-68	One	42	24	8	10	89-55	56	2nd
●		Division One Runners-up					●	
1968-69	One	42	15	12	15	57-53	42	11th
1969-70	One	42	14	17	11	66-61	45	8th
1970-71	One	42	16	11	15	65-66	43	8th
1971-72	One	42	19	10	13	69-61	48	8th
1972-73	One	42	12	13	17	44-60	37	18th
1973-74	One	42	10	12	20	38-48	32	21st
		Relegated						
1974-75	Two	42	26	9	7	66-30	61	1st
★		Division Two Champions					★	
1975-76	One	42	23	10	9	68-42	56	3rd
1976-77	One	42	18	11	13	71-62	47	6th
1977-78	One	42	16	10	16	67-63	42	10th

Season	Division	P	W	D	L	F-A	Pts	Pos
1978-79	One	42	15	15	12	60-63	45	9th
1979-80	One	42	24	10	8	65-35	58	2nd
● **Division One Runners-up** ●								
1980-81	One	42	15	18	9	51-36	48	8th
1981-82	One	42	22	12	8	59-29	78	3rd
1982-83	One	42	19	13	10	56-38	70	3rd
1983-84	One	42	20	14	8	71-41	74	4th
1984-85	One	42	22	10	10	77-47	76	4th
1985-86	One	42	22	10	10	70-36	76	4th
1986-87	One	42	14	14	14	52-45	56	11th
1987-88	One	40	23	12	5	71-38	81	2nd
● **Division One Runners-up** ●								
1988-89	One	38	13	12	13	45-35	51	11th
1989-90	One	38	13	9	16	46-47	48	13th
1990-91	One	38	16	12	10	58-45	59★	6th
1991-92	One	42	21	15	6	63-33	78	2nd
● **Division One Runners-up** ●								
1992-93	Premier	42	24	12	6	67-31	84	1st
★ **Premier League Champions** ★								
1993-94	Premier	42	27	11	4	80-38	92	1st
★ **Premier League Champions** ★								
1994-95	Premier	42	26	10	6	77-28	88	2nd
● **Premier League Runners-up** ●								
1995-96	Premier	38	25	7	6	73-35	82	1st
★ **Premier League Champions** ★								

Season	Division	P	W	D	L	F-A	Pts	Pos
1996–97	Premier	38	21	12	5	76-44	75	1st

★ **Premier League Champions** ★

* point deducted for disciplinary reasons

THROUGH THE YEARS
OCTOBER

1936
October
1

Duncan Edwards was born in Dudley and was destined to become one of the finest players of all time but for the Munich air crash which cost him his life. A stained glass window in celebration of his life and ability can be found in the church at Dudley.

1957
October
11

Robert (Bobby) Charlton was born in Ashington, a member of the famous Milburn family football dynasty. He represented England at schoolboy level and was an integral part of the United youth side which won three FA Youth Cups.

1968
October
16

United played the home leg of the World Club Championship against Estudiantes of Argentina. After the previous month's defeat in Argentina, United were subjected to the most appalling display by their visitors; Bobby Charlton required three stitches after being hacked down, Nobby Stiles was head-butted, Denis Law had to be substituted after having the opposing goalkeeper's studs run down his leg and George Best was punched, kicked and spat upon. Both Nobby Stiles and George Best were sent off, along with Medina of Estudiantes and, although the game ended 1-1, the visitors held on to win the tournament.

1990
October
23

As winners of the FA Cup, United were drawn to play Wrexham, winners of the Welsh FA Cup, in the European Cup Winners' Cup. UEFA rules stated that the visiting club must be in the city where the match was to take place 24 hours prior to kick off, so although the journey from Manchester to Wrexham on the M56 normally takes 40 minutes, United had to set off a day early!

KEEPERS KORNER

Every successful team needs a reliable last line of defence – and though the redoutable Peter Schmeichel has the green jersey at present he's only one of a number of notable United keepers.

 # HARRY GREGG

Ray Wood had begun the 1957-58 season as United's first-choice goalkeeper, but in December of that year Matt Busby put the cat among the pigeons when he swooped to sign Harry Gregg for a then record fee for a goalkeeper, £23,500, in December 1957 from Doncaster Rovers. A 1-0 home defeat against Chelsea early in December was Wood's last game that season, for Gregg seized his chance with both hands.

A survivor of the Munich air crash, as was Wood, Gregg was considered to be in sufficient mental and physical condition immediately after the disaster to play in United's first game, at home to Sheffield Wednesday in the FA Cup. Harry gave an assured and polished performance on an evening already highly emotionally charged and helped United to a 3-0 win.

He played in that season's FA Cup Final, which saw United lose at Wembley for the second season running, although the controversial nature of Nat Lofthouse's second goal for Bolton, in which he bundled Gregg over the line, remains the abiding memory of the day.

That summer Harry went to Sweden with the Northern Irish national side and performed heroics during the World Cup which saw the Irish march to the Quarter-Finals. He was eventually replaced in the national side by Pat Jennings and lost his United place to David Gaskell, subsequently signing for Stoke City and then turning to management with Shrewsbury Town.

HARRY GREGG UNITED APPS 1957-66				
League	FA Cup	League Cup	Europe	Total
210	24	2	11	247

JIMMY RIMMER

If a prophet is without honour in his own country, then Jimmy Rimmer is the home-grown goalkeeper who couldn't find a regular place in the Manchester United first team – even though he'd have walked into most others.

Even so, he didn't do badly. Joining the club from school in 1963, the Southport-born custodian picked up a medal as substitute (unused) in the European Cup Final of 1968. Indeed, he started 1968-69 as first choice in front of Alex Stepney, only to lose his place after two heavy defeats; the two keepers split the 1970-71 season with 20 and 22 appearances respectively, Jimmy an ever-present in the Cups. Rimmer notched 34 League games at Old Trafford in total and, apart from a loan spell at Swansea, was a regular in the squad if not always the team, until leaving for Arsenal in 1974.

As if to prove United had made a major mistake in letting him go, he was the Gunners' Player of the Year in 1975 and made his one and only full England appearance a year later,

against Italy during a tour of the US. Having missed only three League games in as many seasons as Bob Wilson's replacement he was himself replaced by Pat Jennings, making the short trip across London from Spurs – but Rimmer had the last laugh by playing in Aston Villa's Championship-winning team of 1980-81. Unfortunately, injury forced him off the pitch in the 1982 European Cup Final after just ten minutes, giving Nigel Spink his chance to shine. Bet he wished that had happened in '68…

Moving to Swansea, this time permanently, in 1983 Rimmer retired three years later and enjoyed a coaching career thereafter.

JIMMY RIMMER UNITED APPS 1963-74				
League	FA Cup	League Cup	Europe	Total
34	3	6	2	45

 ALEX STEPNEY

Alex Stepney began his career with non-League Tooting and Mitcham before being persuaded to become a professional footballer with Millwall in 1963. Over the next three years he became established as a solid and reliable keeper and Tommy Docherty, then manager at Chelsea, paid £50,000 to take him to Stamford Bridge. Competition from Peter Bonetti restricted him to only one appearance before Matt Busby paid £55,000 to sign him for Manchester United four months later.

He immediately replaced David Gaskell and over the next 12 seasons became a United regular, helping them win the title in his first season and the European Cup the following year, although his England career was restricted to just one appearance.

While the four goals United scored in the European Cup final have since entered folklore, Alex's part in ensuring victory on the evening should not be underestimated. His performance included two exceptional saves in the closing minutes of normal time from Eusebio which kept United in the game. He left United at end of season 1977-78 having collected an FA Cup winner's medal in 1977.

In the 1973-74 relegation season he was appointed United's penalty taker, and when he scored against Birmingham in October of that season his second goal of the season made him joint top-scorer!

ALEX STEPNEY UNITED APPS 1966-78				
League	FA Cup	League Cup	Europe	Total
433	44	35	23	535

GARY BAILEY

Gary Bailey was born in Ipswich but emigrated with his family to South Africa. He was playing university football when recommended to Manchester United for a trial by Eddie Lewis in January 1978.

He made his debut for United in November the same year, against Ipswich, and effectively became first choice until injury forced him into retirement. He made three appearances for United in FA Cup Finals, finishing on the losing side in his first against Arsenal in 1979.

In that game Arsenal had powered into a two-goal lead and appeared to be heading for an easy victory, but late goals from McQueen and McIlroy seemed to have sent the game into extra time. Then a deep cross from Graham Rix eluded Bailey and found Frank Stapleton at the far post for a dramatic winner.

Gary more than made up for this in 1983 when, in extra time against Brighton and with seconds remaining on the clock, he pulled off an exceptional save from Gordon Smith to ensure the game went to a replay. United made no mistake second time around. Smith has since entered folklore as the man who missed a chance to win the Cup for Brighton, but in so doing the save by Gary has been overlooked. Yes, Smith should have scored; the fact that he didn't owed much to the acrobatics of Gary Bailey.

He collected a second winner's medal in 1985 when United prevented Everton from winning a unique Treble, Norman Whiteside's extra-time winner taking the Cup to Old Trafford.

GARY BAILEY UNITED APPS 1976-86				
League	FA Cup	League Cup	Europe	Total
470	54	55	77	656

 # PETER SCHMEICHEL

United's success in winning the 1990 FA Cup and the following season's European Cup Winners' Cup proved to Alex Ferguson one thing; if United were to end their quest for the League title then a world-class goalkeeper was a major requirement.

Immediately after his team had drawn their Cup Final with Crystal Palace, Alex took the momentous decision to drop Scottish keeper Jim Leighton and draft in loan player Les Sealey. While Sealey was still in place for the Cup Winners' Cup Final, United's scouts had been scouring the world for a replacement.

They found one playing in the Danish League for Brondby, and a £550,000 transfer fee secured the services of the 6 foot 4 inch keeper. If there were those who suspected Schmeichel might find stepping up to the Premier League too great a leap, they have been more than pleasantly surprised, for he has undoubtedly become one of the best goalkeepers in the world since arriving at Old Trafford.

A daunting sight for any striker, he has proved able to look after himself should the going get nasty. He is also liable to pop up in the opponents' penalty area looking to add his name to the scoresheet if the situation is looking drastic – his goal in the UEFA Cup a couple of seasons ago was the perfect example for any striker! His sheer enthusiasm for the game should ensure a continuing stream of trophies and titles at Old Trafford for good few years yet.

PETER SCHMEICHEL UNITED APPS 1991-(97)				
League	FA Cup	League Cup	Europe	Total
226	29	17	23	295

BEST SEASON 3

Having relinquished the Premiership title to Blackburn Rovers in a nail biting finish the previous season, United were determined to reclaim the crown in 1995-96.

United started with a 3-1 defeat at Aston Villa on the opening day of the season, leading to many within the media (and one or two among the faithful) to question whether Alex Ferguson was right to put so much faith in the youngsters beginning to break through into the first team. Newcastle quickly surged to the top, with Manchester United slipping into second place, but while in any normal season United's points haul would have soon put them on top, by January Newcastle seemingly had the title all but sown up and a 12 point lead over their rivals.

Fergie has always stated that his team begin to show their true colours come the New Year, but a 4-1 defeat at White Hart Lane was hardly the ideal way to start chipping away at Newcastle. That defeat was the turning point, as United went on an unbeaten run that was to bring them up to Newcastle's shoulder. A vital and morale boosting win at St James' Park (despite being under almost total pressure throughout) handed the impetus to Manchester United, and a draw at QPR took them to the top for the first time that season. Four more straight wins were followed by only the second defeat in the New Year, a 3-1 reverse at Southampton.

Then came the key match, with both Manchester and Newcastle due to play Leeds United. After Manchester United had secured a narrow 1-0 win, Ferguson stated that he hoped the Leeds players, who, in his opinion, had let their manager down throughout the season, would show as much effort in their forthcoming game with Newcastle. All of this was too much for Kevin Keegan; sucked in by Alex's 'mind games' he allowed the pressure to get to him and perhaps showed if Newcastle were to win the League then Manchester had to hand it to them. Straight victories over Nottingham Forest by 5-0 and a final day victory at Middlesbrough showed Manchester United were in no mood to hand the title to anyone other than themselves.

That was not the end of the silverware either, for while the League battle had stretched over 38 games, United had taken the shortest possible route to Wembley for the FA Cup Final and the brink of a second Double. Liverpool performed much below par in the Final and a single strike by Eric Cantona gave United their place in the record books.

1995-96 LEAGUE RECORD

Opponents	Home	Away
Arsenal	1-0	0-1
Aston Villa	0-0	1-3
Blackburn Rovers	1-0	2-1
Bolton Wanderers	3-0	6-0
Chelsea	1-1	4-1
Coventry City	1-0	4-0
Everton	2-0	3-2
Leeds United	1-0	1-3
Liverpool	2-2	0-2
Manchester City	1-0	3-2
Middlesbrough	2-0	3-0
Newcastle United	2-0	1-0
Nottingham Forest	5-0	1-1
Queens Park Rangers	2-1	1-1
Sheffield Wednesday	2-2	0-0
Southampton	4-1	1-3
Tottenham Hotspur	1-0	1-4
West Ham United	2-1	1-0
Wimbledon	3-1	4-2

THROUGH THE YEARS
NOVEMBER

1973
November
29

Wing wizard Ryan Giggs enjoyed his first dribble today in Cardiff – and, despite representing England schoolboys, would go on to represent the country of his birth with distinction, as well as thrilling the Old Trafford faithful.

1986
November
6

The arrival of Alex Ferguson at Old Trafford from Aberdeen, after a temporary spell in charge of Scotland following Jock Stein's untimely death, signalled the beginning of the most successful era since Matt Busby. Not that you'd have realised, initially: it took Alex four seasons to land his first pot!

1989
November
14

Former coach and assistant manager Jimmy Murphy died aged 89. A right-half with West Bromwich Albion before the Second World War, he became coach at Old Trafford at the cessation of hostilities, a post he held for ten years. Elevated to the position of assistant manager in 1955 he was also manager of Wales between 1957 and 1963, a position that perhaps saved his life; he was on World Cup duty with Wales against Israel when the Munich air disaster took place (in fact, Wales had already been eliminated from the competition but, following political boycotts, Israel qualified from their group without playing a single game, a situation FIFA were not prepared to allow. They therefore conducted a draw of group runners-up to provide opposition for Israel – Wales came out of the hat – and he took temporary control of Manchester United whilst Matt Busby was recovering from his injuries. He led a patched up Manchester United to Wembley for the 1958 FA Cup Final and, the same year, took Wales to Sweden for the World Cup finals. He retired as assistant manager of Manchester United in 1971.

1996

November

23

Bryan Robson's reunion with United, as manager of Middlesbrough at the new Riverside Stadium, ended in honours shared, a 2-2 draw. United's seventh position after this result was the lowest they'd occupied during the season: by February '97 they were topping the pile.

GREAT DEFENDERS

United have always been famed for attacking football – but the boys at the back have played their part too. Let's meet five of the very best at keeping the ball out of the net.

 ## BILL FOULKES

Bill Foulkes' achievements for Manchester United are unlikely to ever be beaten, for in today's modern game the chances of a playing career lasting almost 20 years are remote. Freedom of contract, the Bosman ruling and big signing-on fees have meant few players remain with one club that long. And yet Bill Foulkes did all of that, and more.

Born in St Helens on 5 January 1932, he joined United in August 1951, signing from Whiston Boys Club and making his first-team debut in 1952. By 1953 he was a regular and one of the renowned 'Busby Babes' who dominated English football during the mid 1950s. Initially he played right-back, moving later to central defence.

He won one cap for England, against Northern Ireland in 1955, and survived the Munich air disaster of 1958, subsequently becoming (along with Harry Gregg) one of only two players who survived the crash and played in United's next match, the FA Cup tie with Sheffield Wednesday. At the end of the season he captained United in their FA Cup Final against Bolton Wanderers.

Along with Bobby Charlton he was part of the backbone around which Matt Busby rebuilt the side, and a member of the victorious team which won the European Cup in 1968. During his career, with United he won four League titles, an FA Cup and the European Cup and was runner-up twice in the FA Cup.

He retired from playing in 1969 and immediately joined the United backroom staff, although he later coached in both America and Norway. Although Bill scored relatively rarely for United during his career, one of his goals was undoubtedly the most vital in the club's history, for in 1968 he scored the goal that ensured United's passage into the European Cup Final.

BILL FOULKES UNITED RECORD 1952-69									
League		FA Cup		League Cup		Europe		Total	
Apps	Goals	Apps	Goals	Apps	Goals	Apps	Goals	Apps	Goals
566	7	61	—	3	—	52	2	682	9

 # MARTIN BUCHAN

A stylish and classy defender, Martin was able to combine leadership with his skills, and was captain of first club Aberdeen when only 20. The following year he led the Dons to their first Scottish Cup win in 23 years as they beat Celtic 3-1 and a year later was named the Scottish Football Writers' Player of the Year.

After 133 League games, United manager Frank O'Farrell snapped him up for a then bargain fee of £125,000 in March 1972, feeling certain the qualities he had displayed in Scotland could transform a United side that had begun to slip. Although United were subsequently relegated a couple of seasons later, it was Buchan who inspired the side throughout their brief sojourn in the Second Division and ensured a speedy return to the top flight.

In 1977 he captained the side to victory in the FA Cup against Liverpool, in so doing becoming the first man since the war to captain both English and Scottish Cup-winning sides. Having first been capped for Scotland while with Aberdeen, Martin went on to win 34 caps during his career. At the start of the 1983-84 season he joined Oldham Athletic but retired from playing the following season.

MARTIN BUCHAN UNITED RECORD 1972-83									
League		FA Cup		League Cup		Europe		Total	
Apps	Goals	Apps	Goals	Apps	Goals	Apps	Goals	Apps	Goals
376	4	39	—	30	—	10	—	455	4

 # ARTHUR ALBISTON

Arthur Albiston, born on 14 July 1957, arrived from his native Edinburgh to join United as an apprentice in 1972. He made his first-team debut, aged just 17, two years later against arch rivals City in a League Cup tie in front of a packed Old Trafford. But it was England's other famous knock-out competition, the FA Cup, that was to prove the essence of which Albiston's dreams were made.

Still only 19, he was called up to replace injured left-back Stewart Houston for the 1977 FA Cup Final against Liverpool and his first appearance in the competition resulted in a winner's medal as United beat the League Champions 2-1. It was a pivotal point in the young defender's career as he went on to become a regular, if largely unsung, first-team player for ten years.

Quick, nimble and strong in the tackle, Albiston had a sweet left foot and was always happy to turn defence into attack, an ability not unnoticed by Scotland, who capped him at schoolboy, Under-21 and full levels. The peak of Albiston's 14-cap international career was a place in the squad for the 1986 World Cup Finals in Mexico.

Albiston lost his place during 1987 and rejoined his old boss Ron Atkinson at West Brom the following year, but he departed with over 450 appearances under his belt. He appeared in four FA Cup Finals, becoming the first United player to win three winner's medals when Everton's dreams of a unique treble were shattered by Norman Whiteside's extra-time goal in 1985.

ARTHUR ALBISTON UNITED RECORD 1974–88									
League		FA Cup		League Cup		Europe		Total	
Apps	Goals	Apps	Goals	Apps	Goals	Apps	Goals	Apps	Goals
379	6	36	—	37	1	26	—	478	7

 # STEVE BRUCE

Along with Gary Pallister, Steve Bruce formed a partnership at the heart of the United defence that proved to be the launchpad for League title success, for his arrival at Old Trafford in 1987 coincided with an upswing in United's fortunes.

Born in Corbridge on 31 December 1960, he began his career with Gillingham, signing as an apprentice in 1978 and going on to make nearly 250 appearances for the Gills before joining Norwich for £125,000 in 1984. He enjoyed three seasons with the Canaries, culminating with membership of the side that won the Milk Cup in 1985 against Sunderland and the Second Division Championship in 1986 before an £800,000 switch to United.

After a barren three years the trophy room began to fill up, and, by the time Bruce was given a free transfer in 1996, he had helped United win three League titles, the League Cup, two FA Cups, the European Cup Winners' Cup and three Charity Shields as well as the European Super Cup. The only surprise is that he was never selected for the full England side, having only one England B cap to his name.

At the end of the 1995-96 season Steve Bruce joined Birmingham City, although there had been considerable speculation throughout his last season with United that any number of clubs were willing to make him player-manager. He is sure to pursue a career in management somewhere along the line.

STEVE BRUCE UNITED RECORD 1987-96

League		FA Cup		League Cup		Europe		Total	
Apps	Goals	Apps	Goals	Apps	Goals	Apps	Goals	Apps	Goals
309	36	41	3	34	6	29	7	413	52

 # GARY PALLISTER

A series of highly polished performances for Middlesbrough throughout the 1988-89 season made Gary Pallister a target for just about every major club in the country. Born in Ramsgate on 30 June 1965, he began his career in non-League football with Billingham Town and was soon spotted by Middlesbrough, who secured his services on a free transfer in 1984. He was briefly loaned out to local rivals Darlington in order to get League experience, and when he returned to Ayresome Park was already on his way to becoming the finished article.

He made nearly 200 appearances for Middlesbrough, with a host of scouts soon flocking to see him in action. They saw a fast-paced, stylish defender seldom beaten in the air, able to distribute the ball quickly and accurately and also able to pose a threat at set pieces. United paid £2.3 million to obtain his services and he quickly formed an exciting partnership with Steve Bruce.

Since Bruce's departure Gary has linked with Ronny Johnsen, among others, but the truth of the matter is that Pallister can combine with almost anyone to form an effective obstacle for strikers. During his time at Old Trafford he has been an integral part of the club that has lifted four League titles, three FA Cups, the European Cup Winners' Cup, the League Cup and four Charity Shields, and Gary has also won 22 caps for England and is an essential part of Glenn Hoddle's squad for the World Cup campaign in France '98.

GARY PALLISTER UNITED RECORD 1989-(97)									
League		FA Cup		League Cup		Europe		Total	
Apps	Goals	Apps	Goals	Apps	Goals	Apps	Goals	Apps	Goals
284	12	35	1	36	—	35	1	390	14

THE WAR YEARS

Although the First World War broke out in 1914, the Football League continued unchanged for one more season before regional leagues were organised, the original intention being to maintain morale at home.

United spent the entire season battling against relegation from the First Division and finally secured their status thanks to a 1-0 win at home to Aston Villa, finishing the season in 18th position and seemingly condemning Chelsea and Spurs to relegation. However, already trouble was brewing, as it was alleged and subsequently proven that the result of the 2 April fixture against Liverpool, a 2-0 win for United, had been fixed by several players from both sides.

A rash of betting in and around Manchester and Liverpool on the result being 2-0 had alerted the bookies and they subsequently passed on their doubts to the authorities. Four players from both sides were subsequently banned from the game and, when League football resumed in 1919 and the League was enlarged, the unsavoury nature of United's win and its implications for Chelsea were noted and the latter were not relegated to the Second Division. Spurs, however, were, and their place was given to Arsenal, thus sparking intense north London rivalry!

When the Second World War broke out in 1939, regional football was again organised with United competing in the Western Division. As with most other clubs, numerous players were called up for duty in the armed forces and the club often had to enlist the help of guests in order to put out a full team. Among the more notable players United used during the conflict were Len Butt of Blackburn Rovers and Tommy Woodward of Bolton.

Sometimes even fielding a team was a problem – in one game Blackburn had to enlist four volunteers from the crowd in order to field an 11 against United at Stockport. Not surprisingly, United won 9-0. In keeping with most clubs, however, the full line-ups were not always made official, for if German spies had noticed that Stanley Matthews had played for United they would also know the whereabouts of his army unit!

Of course, the most obvious effect of the Second World War was the extensive bomb damage suffered at Old Trafford and the necessity for the club to move to Maine Road to share with City. At the end of the war adventurous plans were discussed which would take Old Trafford's capacity well beyond 100,000 – but, with building materials still rationed and United having to pay 'rent' to City of £5,000 and a percentage of receipts, the eventual rebuilding work was little more than patching up the damage as best as they could.

GAFFERSPEAK

The word from the Old Trafford manager's office – wit, wisdom and warmth.

'Sir Matt's greatest achievement was that he made United a way of life for people. He made Old Trafford a magical place.'
Bobby Charlton on Busby

'We have been winning through the 1990s. Now there is the pain of defeat, and it's showing. It was good to see that. Sometimes the players forget what losing is like…the experience can help the team develop.' *Alex Ferguson*

'I can meet ministers and monarchs and my children are not much impressed, but when we met Alex Ferguson they realised there was some point to my job.'
Prime Minister Tony Blair

'To be honest, I suppose I wasn't sane. I was raving and creating hell with everyone. Why us? Was it some human error, or had it been decreed from above? If so, why hadn't I died with them? What was so special about me that I'd survived?' *Matt Busby remembers Munich*

'Mark Hughes is a warrior you could trust with your life.'
Alex Ferguson on 'Sparky'

'Matt Busby was the first tracksuit manager, a psychologist, an inspirational leader of men.' *Jackie Blanchflower*

'You see Fergie on the touchline nowadays and he's laughing and smiling. It's like watching a fan who's having a great time.'
Former player Paddy Crerand

'I've had to swop my Merc for a BMW, I'm down to my last 37 suits and I'm drinking non-vintage champagne.'
Ron Atkinson says goodbye to Old Trafford

'Norman Whiteside's not only a good player, but spiteful in the best sense of the word.' *High praise from Ron Atkinson*

'I did not set out to build a team: the task ahead was much bigger. What I really embarked upon was the building of a system which would produce not one but four or five teams, the summit of which was the first XI.' *Matt Busby, 1958*

'I've always said there's a place for the press, but they haven't dug it yet.' *Tommy Docherty*

'These youngsters are the best I've had in my managerial career. A lot of people tell me they could be the best the club has ever had. Now it's just a matter of fitting them into the first team when the opportunity arises.'
Alex Ferguson on the class of '92

'Greatness is doing things that are different; things the ordinary player cannot do.' *Matt Busby*

'I believe you are seeking a team manager? Well, I am interested.'
Matt Busby's first words at Old Trafford, 1945

'Every signing you make is a gamble. But look at Andy's goal record. Some people would pay £10 million for that.'
Alex Ferguson on bagging Cole

THROUGH THE YEARS
DECEMBER

1931

December

26

Christmas is always associated with stuffing, but the 7–0 defeat Wolves handed out to the Red Devils was their second such scoreline in almost exactly a year. 27 December 1930 had seen them lose by an identical margin to another Midlands side, Aston Villa: maybe too much turkey was the problem!

1941

December

31

Manager Alex Ferguson is born in Glasgow. He shares his birthday, albeit 19 years earlier, with former captain Steve Bruce, who was to make his entrance slightly further south in Newcastle. The pair's double act would ring in many happy new years in the 1990s.

1963
December
8

Striker cum midfield man Brian McClair, who joined United in 1987 from Celtic, was born in Bellshill. The Glasgow suburb also gave the football world one Ally McCoist, so maybe they put something in the water!

1972
December
19

George Best announces his retirement from football in a letter to Manchester United. This happens on the same day United sack manager Frank O'Farrell, coach Malcolm Musgrove and chief scout John Aston.

1996
December
21

A 5-0 thrashing of Sunderland, continental strikers Solskjaer and Cantona each scoring twice, powers United nearer the top of the table. Their best win of the season leaves them in fifth place: the Wearsiders, by contrast, will end 18th and be relegated.

THE KITBAG

Few clubs have attracted as much publicity over changes of strip as Manchester United.

While the name on those red shirts has remained constant over the last decade or so (their sponsors are electrical manufacturers Sharp), the kit has changed both design and colour on seemingly a regular basis.

The home shirt has always been red, but subtle changes in the collar design (button-down, retro-style laces, etc) have ensured a steady stream of customers to the United shop looking to buy the latest issue. That stream, however, has been a torrent when the away kit has to be purchased, for United have often gone through a season with not one but two, sometimes three away strips. One such strip even nostalgically recalled the club's previous incarnation as Newton Heath, for United introduced a green and yellow kit similar to that which their ancestors wore on the mudflats of Monsall and Clayton.

There have been black kits, white kits, grey kits, blue and white vertical stripes; almost every colour of the rainbow has figured in the United kit of the 1990s. Some might see this as a not–too–subtle way of getting their customers to part with a regular small fortune – but, as has often been pointed out, a football shirt is an important fashion item of the decade, even if the strip itself only lasts for one season, and few other items of clothing enjoy quite as much exposure and regular wear.

Of course, United are responsible for perhaps one of the funniest episodes in football history when, at half time during a heavy beating at Southampton, Alex Ferguson instructed his team to change their grey away shirts because he later claimed his players could not see their team-mates against the crowd! The new shirts did little better, for United still lost…but in an instant a classic story was born.

EUROPEAN CUP

The ultimate prize and Alex Ferguson's quest – so follow in Busby's footsteps. Here are the stats.

Stage	Opponents	Home	Away	Agg
1956-57				
Prelim	Anderlecht	10-0	2-0	12-0
Round 1	Borussia Dortmund	3-2	0-0	3-2
Quarter-Final	Atletico Bilbao	3-0	3-5	6-5
Semi-Final	Real Madrid	2-2	1-3	3-5
1957-58				
Prelim	Shamrock Rovers	3-2	6-0	9-2
Round 1	Dukla Prague	3-0	0-1	3-1
Quarter-Final	Red Star Belgrade	2-1	3-3	5-4
Semi-Final	AC Milan	2-1	0-4	2-5
1965-66				
Prelim	HJ Helsinki	6-0	3-2	9-2
Round 1	Vorwaerts Berlin	3-1	2-0	5-1
Quarter-Final	Benfica	3-2	5-1	8-3
Semi-Final	Partizan Belgrade	1-0	0-2	1-2

Stage	Opponents	Home	Away	Agg
	1967-68			
Round 1	Hibernian	4-0	0-0	4-0
Round 2	Sarajevo	2-1	0-0	2-1
Quarter-Final	Gornik Zabrze	2-0	0-1	2-1
Semi-Final	Real Madrid	1-0	3-3	4-3
Final	Benfica	—	—	4-1
	1968-69			
Round 1	Waterford	7-1	3-1	10-2
Round 2	Anderlecht	3-0	1-3	4-3
Quarter-Final	Rapid Vienna	3-0	0-0	3-0
Semi-Final	AC Milan	1-0	0-2	1-2
	1993-94			
Round 1	Kispest Honved	2-1	3-2	5-3
Round 2	Galatasaray	3-3	0-0	3-3

United lost on away goals

Stage	Opponents	Home	Away	Agg
	1994-95			
Group A	IFK Gothenburg	4-2	—	—
Group A	Galatasaray	—	0-0	—
Group A	Barcelona	2-2	—	—
Group A	Barcelona	—	0-4	—
Group A	IFK Gothenburg	—	1-3	—
Group A	Galatasaray	4-0	—	—

United failed to qualify for the knockout stages

Stage	Opponents	Home	Away	Agg
1996-97				
Group C	Juventus	—	0-1	—
Group C	Rapid Vienna	2-0	—	—
Group C	Fenerbahce	—	2-0	—
Group C	Fenerbahce	0-1	—	—
Group C	Juventus	0-1	—	—
Group C	Rapid Vienna	—	2-0	—
Quarter-Final	Porto	4-0	0-0	4-0
Semi-Final	Borussia Dortmund	0-1	0-1	0-2

EUROPEAN CUP WINNERS' CUP

This competition gave Alex Ferguson's side their first taste of European glory. Here is the complete ECWC record.

Stage	Opponents	Home	Away	Agg
1963-64				
Round 1	Tilburg Willem II	6-1	1-1	7-2
Round 2	Tottenham Hotspur	4-1	0-2	4-3
Quarter-Final	Sporting Lisbon	4-1	0-5	4-6
1977-78				
Round 1	St Etienne	2-0	1-1	3-1
Round 2	Porto	5-2	0-4	5-6
1983-84				
Round 1	Dukla Prague	1-1	2-2	3-3
	United won on away goals			
Round 2	Spartak Varna	2-0	2-1	4-1
Quarter-Final	Barcelona	3-0	0-2	3-2
Semi-Final	Juventus	1-1	1-2	2-3

Stage	Opponents	Home	Away	Agg
1990-91				
Round 1	Pesci Munkas	2-0	1-0	3-0
Round 2	Wrexham	3-0	2-0	5-0
Quarter-Final	Montpellier	1-1	2-0	3-1
Semi-Final	Legia Warsaw	1-1	3-1	4-2
Final	Barcelona	—	—	2-1
1991-92				
Round 1	Athinaikos	2-0	0-0	2-0
Round 2	Atletico Madrid	1-1	0-3	1-4

INTER-CITIES FAIRS/UEFA CUP

United have never reached the Final of this competition, though Peter Schmeichel did score in 1995–96 in an attempt to progress.

Stage	Opponents	Home	Away	Agg
1964-65				
Round 1	Djurgaaden	6-1	1-1	7-2
Round 2	Borussia Dortmund	4-0	6-1	10-1
Round 3	Everton	1-1	2-1	3-2
Quarter-Final	Racing Strasbourg	0-0	5-0	5-0
Semi-Final	Ferencvaros	3-2	0-1	3-3
United lost the replay 1-2				
1976-77				
Round 1	Ajax	2-0	0-1	2-1
Round 2	Juventus	1-0	0-3	1-3
1980-81				
Round 1	Widzew Lodz	1-1	0-0	1-1
United lost on away goals				
1982-83				
Round 1	Valencia	0-0	1-2	1-2

Stage	Opponents	Home	Away	Agg
	1984-85			
Round 1	Raba Gyor	3-0	2-2	5-2
Round 2	PSV Eindhoven	1-0	0-0	1-0
Round 3	Dundee United	2-2	3-2	5-4
Quarter-Final	Videoton	1-0	0-1	1-1
	United lost 4-5 on penalties			
	1992-93			
Round 1	Torpedo Moscow	0-0	0-0	0-0
	United lost 3-4 on penalties			
	1995-96			
Round 1	Rotor Volgograd	2-2	0-0	2-2
	United lost on away goals			

United's record against European opposition

Country	P	W	D	L	F-A
Austria	4	3	1	—	7-0
Belgium	4	3	—	1	16-3
Bulgaria	2	2	—	—	4-1
Czechoslovakia	4	1	2	1	6-4
East Germany	2	2	—	—	5-1
Eire	4	4	—	—	19-4
England	4	2	1	1	7-5
Finland	2	2	—	—	9-2
France	6	3	3	—	11-2
Germany (inc West)	6	3	1	2	13-5
Greece	2	1	1	—	2-0
Holland	6	3	2	1	10-3
Hungary	11	7	1	3	18-11
Italy	10	3	1	6	6-15
Malta	2	1	1	—	4-0
Poland	6	2	3	1	7-4
Portugal	9	6	1	2	25-16
Russia	4	—	4	—	2-2
Scotland	2	1	1	—	5-4
Spain	15	4	5	6	22-28
Sweden	4	2	1	1	12-7
Turkey	6	2	3	1	9-4
Wales	2	2	—	—	5-0
Yugoslavia	6	3	2	1	8-7

SUBSTITUTES

As you'd expect for a man who picks a different team for each occasion, Alex Ferguson is a canny player of the substitute system.

Whether he can name three for League action, five for FA Cup or more for Europe, he's certain to give himself the widest possible range of options. These usually include a keeper – and an incident in November 1994 showed the wisdom of that tactic – for when Peter Schmeichel ricked his back in the warm-up, Fergie could pull Kevin Pilkington off the bench when the Dane admitted defeat after eight minutes' play. It was the youngster's debut but he starred in a 3-0 win…his only game of the season.

Some of the biggest names have warmed the bench, not just recently (Andy Cole comes to mind) but in the past. Two Scots internationals, Lou Macari and latterly Brian McClair, have spent a good deal of time looking on: Macari was labelled 'The Judge' so often was he seen on the bench!

Youngsters have found the substitute's role a way in to first-team contention, and Fergie has found that blooding them gradually is the best way to bring his fledglings to full flight. The 1994-95 season for instance saw Paul Scholes and Nicky Butt both make 11 appearances as sub, in Butt's case as many as he started: his previous two showings in the League had both been from the bench. And the great David Beckham made his first-team debut as a sub in the Third Round of the Coca-Cola Cup against Brighton in 1992, fully two years before he got his League nod.

'Becks' had replaced flying winger Andre Kanchelskis on that occasion, and repeated the trick in the 1995 FA Cup Quarter and Semi-Finals. The Russian, who himself had starred as a sub in 1992-93 with some match-winning performances, was not best pleased and, seeing future opportunities limited, was soon off to Everton. Another forward who felt the indignity of being substituted was Peter Beardsley. Subbed at half-time in his only game for United, he left the club to make his name elsewhere!

In the 1980s, Mark Robins (now with Leicester) became something of a supersub. A young player who couldn't claim a regular place, his speed would often make a much-needed breakthrough after he was introduced into the final stages of a game: without him, the 1990 FA Cup win that gave Alex Ferguson his first taste of silverware at Old Trafford (and arguably kept him his job) would have foundered at the very first hurdle. Wins against Nottingham Forest and, in the Semi-Final replay, Oldham, were both obtained courtesy of Robins strikes. Unfortunately Palace, their opponents in the Final, had an equally potent supersub in two-goal Ian Wright, but United won through after a replay.

As previously mentioned, £7 million man Andy Cole played a role as sub before claiming a regular place in the team – few managers but Alex Ferguson would dare play a record signing for only part of a match, but the tactic worked and Cole, his confidence restored, is now a regular. The striker also made his England bow from the bench against Uruguay in 1991 – and rattled the bar!

At the end of the day, warming the Old Trafford bench is surely the equal of being a first-teamer anywhere else. It's so often the stepping stone to a regular place, and with Fergie willing to use his options you'll rarely be left picking up splinters for 90 minutes. What's more, with the famous backsides which have taken their place there, it can only be a matter of time before the dugout gets a blue plaque!

DREAM TEAM 3

After a 26-year wait United were finally able to bring home the League title in 1992-93 and thus resume their quest for the European Cup. The bulk of this side is still in place and continues the hunt for silverware on both the domestic and European fronts.

SCHMEICHEL 1

PARKER 2 · PALLISTER 6 · BRUCE 5 · IRWIN 3

McCLAIR 9 · INCE 8 · KEANE 4 · GIGGS 11

HUGHES 10 · CANTONA 7

Goalkeeper   **Peter Schmeichel**

Probably the best goalkeeper in the world at present, it was his imposing presence that turned United into a formidable unit. Joined United for £550,000 from Brondby in 1991 and has since won every domestic honour with his club.

Right-back   **Paul Parker**

Joined United in 1991 for £2 million, having given both Fulham and QPR exceptional service and having broken into the England side. Enjoyed five highly successful years at Old Trafford before moving on to Derby on a free transfer, later playing for Sheffield United, Fulham (second spell), Chelsea and a number of non-League clubs.

Left-back   **Denis Irwin**

One of the unsung heroes of the United side, his career at Old Trafford has shown him to be a model of consistency. Began his career with Leeds but was released in 1986, subsequently signing for United from Oldham in 1990 for £625,000.

Central defender   **Steve Bruce**

Began his career with Gillingham and Norwich before switching to Old Trafford for £800,000 in 1987. He then went on to win three League titles, one League Cup (to go with previous success in the competition at Norwich), two FA Cups and the European Cup Winners' Cup. The only surprise is that he did not collect international honours. Joined Birmingham City on a free transfer in 1996.

Midfielder   **Brian McClair**
Launched his professional career with Motherwell before signing for Celtic in 1983, switching to Old Trafford in 1987. Although now a squad member rather than a regular in the side, he can always be relied upon to serve the cause.

Central defender   **Gary Pallister**
A mobile stopper, Gary has proven to be one of the best readers of the game for both club and country, collecting 22 England caps as well as medals galore for United. Has overcome a number of injuries during his career.

Midfielder   **Eric Cantona**
An inspirational figure both on and off the field, he won League title medals in three consecutive seasons, one for Leeds and then two for United. Five titles in six seasons is indicative of his influence.

Midfielder   **Paul Ince**
The self-styled Guv'nor of the midfield area for both club and

country, Paul blossomed at Old Trafford into probably the first name manager Alex Ferguson put on his team sheet. Began his career with West Ham.

Midfielder   Roy Keane
Along with Ince, Roy Keane provided the engine to Manchester United's midfield; a tough-tackling, no-nonsense performer who set up many of the attacks that provided United with their Championship wins. He began his career with Nottingham Forest in 1990 and switched to United in 1993 for £3.75 million.

Striker   Mark Hughes
Enjoyed two highly successful spells at Old Trafford, either side of a brief stay with crack Spanish side Barcelona. There are those who are convinced Ferguson may have let him leave Old Trafford too early; certainly his form at Chelsea still shows him to be a feared striker.

Midfielder   Ryan Giggs
One of the most talented players in the British game, he made his United breakthrough in 1991 and has since become an integral part of the side. He has won four Premiership titles, two FA Cups and a League Cup medal – all before his 24th birthday. Having put a series of injuries behind him, he was leading United's charge for a hat-trick of titles in 1997-98.

WORST SEASON 3

If the 1950s and 1960s had been United's golden age, then the 1970s began with the club on a slide. Having had stability for so long, the effects of three managers in the space of four seasons soon began to take effect.

The club appointed Tommy Docherty in December 1972, hoping that his flamboyant manner would work a miracle at the club. In his first few months so it did, for although they had hovered around the relegation zone for much of the 1972–73 campaign, a late revival lifted them clear and promised better things the following season.

In truth, the odds were stacked against United and Docherty for the 1973–74 season. Bobby Charlton and Denis Law had played their last games for United, although Denis in particular would have one more appearance at Old Trafford, while George Best had entered into his troubled period, announcing his retirement.

Docherty's new–look side didn't start too badly, with two wins in the opening three games (against Stoke and QPR), but only three wins between then and Christmas saw the club plummet down the table. United saw the year out with a 2-0 victory over Ipswich, but bottom of the table.

The New Year began in much the same fashion as the old; three draws and four defeats in the next seven games looked to have condemned them, but a brief revival of four wins and two draws gave a lifeline. With three games left, United could still save themselves, but victory was vital.

It was not to be, as defeat at Everton left United in real danger of going down to the Second Division for the first time in 37 years. On the final Saturday of the season, Old Trafford was packed with 56,996 to see whether United could avoid the drop or if City were the team to send them down.

A tense display by United did not auger well, and as time slipped by it seemed as though a goalless draw would be the outcome, a result which would still relegate the Red Devils. Then, with some five minutes left, Law casually backheeled the ball past Alex Stepney, the crowd invaded the pitch and the match was abandoned. The League later ordered the result to stand, confirming United's relegation.

Even victory would not have saved United, for defeat at Stoke two days later left them four points adrift of safety.

1973-74 LEAGUE RECORD

Opponents	Home	Away
Arsenal	1-1	0-3
Birmingham City	1-0	0-1
Burnley	3-3	0-0
Chelsea	2-2	3-1
Coventry City	2-3	0-1
Derby County	0-1	2-2
Everton	3-0	0-1
Ipswich Town	2-0	1-2
Leeds United	0-2	0-0
Leicester City	1-2	0-1
Liverpool	0-0	0-2
Manchester City	0-1	0-0
Newcastle United	1-0	2-3
Norwich City	0-0	2-0
Queens Park Rangers	2-1	0-3
Sheffield United	1-2	1-0
Southampton	0-0	1-1
Stoke City	1-0	0-1
Tottenham Hotspur	0-1	1-2
West Ham United	3-1	1-2
Wolverhampton Wanderers	0-0	1-2

UNITED'S ALL-TIME ROLL OF HONOUR

1896-97	Division Two Runners-up
1905-06	Division Two Runners-up
1907-08	Division One Champions
1908-09	FA Cup Winners
1910-11	Division One Champions
1924-25	Division Two Runners-up
1935-36	Division Two Champions
1937-38	Division Two Runners-up
1946-47	Division One Runners-up
1947-48	Division One Runners-up and FA Cup Winners
1948-49	Division One Runners-up
1950-51	Division One Runners-up
1951-52	Division One Champions
1955-56	Division One Champions
1956-57	Division One Champions and FA Cup Runners-up
1957-58	FA Cup Runners-up
1958-59	Division One Runners-up
1962-63	FA Cup Winners
1963-64	Division One Runners-up
1964-65	Division One Champions
1966-67	Division One Champions
1967-68	Division One Runners-up, European Cup Winners and World Club Championship Runners-up

1974-75	Division Two Champions
1975-76	FA Cup Runners-up
1976-77	FA Cup Winners
1978-79	FA Cup Runners-up
1979-80	Division One Runners-up
1982-83	FA Cup Winners and League Cup Runners-up
1984-85	FA Cup Winners
1987-88	Division One Runners-up
1989-90	FA Cup Winners
1990-91	League Cup Runners-up, European Cup Winners' Cup Winners and Super Cup Winners
1991-92	Division One Runners-up and League Cup Winners
1992-93	Premier League Champions
1993-94	Premier League Champions, FA Cup Winners and League Cup Runners-up
1994-95	Premier League Runners-up and FA Cup Runners-up
1995-96	Premier League Champions and FA Cup Winners
1996-97	Premier League Champions

QUIZ ANSWERS

See page 122–125 for questions.

1   Real Madrid

2   Charlton Athletic

3   Sheffield Wednesday in the FA Cup Fifth Round.

4   Rotor Volgograd

5   1908–09

6   1907–08

7   76,962 for Wolves v Grimsby in the
     1939 FA Cup Semi-Final.

8   70,504 v Aston Villa, League Division One on
     27 December 1920.

9   Peter Reid of Everton

10   Nottingham Forest 1-0

11   1966–67 against Blackpool (lost 5-1).

12   Three – 1985, 1990 and 1994.

13   'Come On You Reds' in 1994

14   1974–75

15   Red Star Belgrade

16   Chelsea and Derby

17   Newcastle United, Southampton and Sunderland

18	14
19	4 – 1982, 1983, 1984 and 1986.
20	Crystal Palace in 1909
21	21
22	Eric Cantona in 1996.
23	Eric Cantona in 1994.
24	1992 and 1991.
25	George Best in 1968.
26	Eric Cantona on 6 December 1992.
27	11
28	Sunderland
29	Newcastle United
30	Rai Van der Gouw
31	Spurs (United won 5-0)
32	Mark Hughes with two
33	11
34	Bobby Charlton (two), George Best and Brian Kidd
35	Anderlecht
36	Six
37	Manchester City 2 Manchester United 3
38	Middlesbrough
39	103 in 1956-57 and 1958-59
40	Dennis Viollet, 32 in season 1959-60.

THE LAST WORD

'A Manchester United player has to want the ball, have the courage to want the ball. He's a player with imagination, someone who has the big picture.'

Alex Ferguson